D0467077

THE CIVILIZATION
OF ANGKOR

By the same author

The Archaeology of Mainland Southeast Asia
The Bronze Age of Southeast Asia
Prehistoric Thailand

THE CIVILIZATION
OF ANGKOR

Charles Higham

Weidenfeld & Nicolson

LONDON

First published in Great Britain in 2001
by Weidenfeld & Nicolson

© 2001 Charles Higham
The moral right of Charles Higham to be identified as the author
of this work has been asserted by him in accordance with
the Copyright, Designs and Patents Act of 1988.

All rights reserved. No part of this publication may be reproduced,
stored in a retrieval system, or transmitted
in any form or by any means, electronic, mechanical,
photocopying, recording, or otherwise, without the prior
permission of both the copyright owner and the above
publisher of this book.

A CIP catalogue record for this book is available
from the British Library.

ISBN 0 297 82457 0

Typeset by Selwood Systems, Midsomer Norton

Printed in Great Britain by
Butler & Tanner Ltd, Frome and London

Weidenfeld & Nicolson

The Orion Publishing Group Ltd
Orion House
5 Upper Saint Martin's Lane
London WC2H 9EA

Contents

ILLUSTRATIONS

A rare scene from the Bayon showing a family following the army on
the march

Jayavarman VII's magnificent bridge over the Chikreng River

Servants preparing food for a feast in a bas-relief from the Bayon

The Chams in their highly-decorated galleys on the Great Lake

A game of chess in a quiet corner at the Bayon

A woman in childbirth attended by three midwives under the shade of
a wooden pavilion

The Bayon temple, Madhyadri, in the centre of Angkor Thom

Two men preparing to release their fighting boars

ACKNOWLEDGEMENTS

Any attempt to understand and describe the civilization of Angkor inevitably confronts a wide range of source material which no scholar can hope to be familiar with at first hand. This study is no exception. Virtually all the information on the earliest origins of Angkor comes from archaeological research on prehistoric sites. While archaeology continues to be a potential source of data into the historic period, it is amplified by Sanskrit and Khmer inscriptions, art history and Chinese documents. One result of this maze of source material is that embedded opinions are commonly reiterated in so many layers that they take on the status of dogma.

Michael Vickery has stressed this point with particular reference to the seventh- and eighth-century Old Khmer inscriptions: it is vital, he says, to return critically to the original and contemporary sources. This study has followed his precept in incorporating, wherever possible, the inscriptions that date to the reign under review, linked to their geographical distribution. Being illiterate in Sanskrit or Khmer, I have relied on the French translations by Georges Cœdès and Claude Jacques as well as commentaries by Vickery. Archaeological research on historic sites has barely begun, but the recent excavations in the Mekong Delta by Miriam Stark, Pierre-Yves Manguin and Vo Si Khai have shown the huge potential of this discipline.

I am most grateful to Rachanie Thosarat, my co-director on the excavations of Noen U-Loke, and Dougald O'Reilly, who excavated Non Muang Kao as part of our project 'The Origins of the Civilization of Angkor'. The text of Chapter 4 would have been very different in content had I not had access to Michael Vickery's seminal volume on the economy and social institutions of the seventh and eighth centuries. I record here my indebtedness to him for a most helpful exchange of views in Phnom Penh and for his comments on reading a draft of this book. I also thank Masako Marui for providing illustrations of Ishanapura, and HE Vann Molyvann and Ang Choulean for their encouragement and assistance in undertaking research on Angkor. Most generously, Miriam Stark, Pierre-Yves Manguin and Vo Si Khai also made available material from their fieldwork prior to publication. Pascal Rovère kindly escorted me over the Baphuon Temple when it was closed for reconstruction under his supervision. HE Janos Jelen of the Royal Angkor Foundation and Elizabeth Moore have been generous with advice and help in many ways.

I would like to record my indebtedness to the Master and Fellows of St Catharine's College, Cambridge, for electing me as a visiting scholar during 1999, and to Professor Lord Renfrew of Kaimsthorn and his colleagues of the McDonald Institute in the University of Cambridge for providing me with a visiting fellowship during the writing of this study.

Finally, I thank the staff at Weidenfeld and Nicolson for their sympathetic encouragement and advice.

TIMELINE

2300–2000 BC The arrival of rice farming communities in Cambodia, ultimately from the Yangzi Valley, bringing the early Khmer Language; main site in Cambodia is Samrong Sen

circa 2000 BC The construction of Stonehenge

1500–500 BC The Bronze Age of South-East Asia

500 BC–AD 400 The period known as the Iron Age of South-East Asia; key sites include Noen U-Loke and Angkor Borei

AD 60–1 Boudicca revolts against Roman occupation of Britain

AD 122 The construction of Hadrian's Wall begins

AD 150–550 The rise and fall of the delta state known as Funan; the sites of Oc Eo and Angkor Borei occupied

AD 410 The fall of the Western Roman Empire

510 The death of Jayavarman of Funan and the accession of Rudravarman

597 St Augustine is sent by Pope Gregory the Great to England

600 Mahendravarman assumes kingship of a polity in central Cambodia

615–28 The reign of Ishanavarman I at Ishanapura

655–700 The approximate reign of Jayavarman I and the construction of the Ak Yum temple

703 The Venerable Bede is ordained a priest at Jarrow

793 The Vikings' first raid on England, at Lindisfarne

800 The coronation of Charlemagne

802 The traditional date for the consecration of Jayavarman II as king of kings, and the foundation of the kingdom of Angkor

871 Alfred the Great becomes King of England

877 Indravarman I becomes king; the Bakhong and Preah Ko temples constructed at Hariharalaya

889 The accession of Yashovarman I; the Bakheng temple constructed; the Lolei completed; the Eastern Baray and the Indratataka finished

928 The accession of Jayavarman IV and the establishment of the capital at Lingapura, Koh Ker

935 The death of King Canute

944 The accession of Rajendravarman; construction of Pre Rup and the Eastern Mebon

968–1000 The reign of Jayavarman V; the Ta Keo temple constructed but never finished

1002 Civil war between Suryavarman I and Jayaviravarman; the construction of the Western Baray commences about this period

1042 Edward the Confessor crowned the last king of Anglo-Saxon England

1050 The accession of Udayadityavarman II and the construction of the Baphuon

1066 The Battle of Hastings

1080 The foundation of the dynasty of Mahidharapura under Jayavarman VI; the temple of Phimai built

1099 The army of the First Crusade encamps before Jerusalem

1113 The accession of Suryavarman II

1140 The construction of Angkor Wat under way

1154 Nicolas Breakspear becomes the first English pope, Adrian IV

1177 Angkor is sacked by a Cham army

1170 The murder of Thomas à Becket in Canterbury Cathedral

1181 The beginning of the construction of Angkor Thom, the Bayon, the Jayatataka, Preah Khan and Ta Prohm

1192 Richard I, the Lionheart, taken prisoner

1215 Magna Carta is signed

1220 The death of Jayavarman VII

1296 The visit of Zhou Daguan to Angkor during the reign of
   Indravarman III

1415 The Battle of Agincourt

1431 The traditional date for the abandonment of Angkor after a
   Thai invasion

1455–85 The Wars of the Roses, York against Lancaster

1550–1600 The first Portuguese visitors to Angkor

1588 The Spanish Armada sails; William Shakespeare begins
   writing

For
Joseph and Miriam as they embark on a great adventure
Alexandra and Kate
Louis and Charles

CHAPTER I

INTRODUCTION: 'ONE OF THE MARVELS OF THE WORLD'

During the sixteenth century, barely a hundred and fifty years after it had been abandoned, Portuguese traders and missionaries became aware of a great stone city hidden deep in the forests of northern Cambodia. They had come upon temples where a much older religion than theirs had flourished, a sacred city, which included the largest of all religious monuments. Reaching up through the jungle canopy, the five lotus towers of Angkor Wat would have inspired awe then as they do now. One of the first visitors was Antonio da Magdalena, a Capuchin friar, who explored the ruined city in 1586. Three years later, he gave Diogo do Couto, the official historian of the Portuguese Indies, an account of his visit and then, sadly, lost his life when shipwrecked off the coast of Natal in 1589. Do Couto, however, set down the friar's recollections thus:

> This city is square, with four principal gates, and a fifth which serves the royal palace. The city is surrounded by a moat, crossed by five bridges. These have on each side a cordon held by giants. Their ears are all pierced and are very long. The stone blocks of the bridges are of astonishing size. The stones of the walls are of an extraordinary size and so jointed together that they look as if they are made of just one stone. The gates of each entrance are magnificently sculpted, so perfect, so delicate that Antonio da Magdalena, who was in this city, said that they looked as if they were made from one stone the source of which is, amazingly, over 20 leagues away. So you can judge the labour and organisation dedicated to

construction. There are written lines which record that this city, these temples, and other things were built by the order of 20 kings over a period of 700 years. On the sides of this city are monuments which must be royal palaces on account of their sumptuous decoration and grandeur. In the middle of the city is an extraordinary temple. From each of the gates, there is a causeway of the same width as the bridges, flanked by canals, fed by the great moat round the city. The water originates from the north and east, and leaves from the south and west. The system is fed by the river diverted there. Half a league from this city is a temple called Angar. It is of such extraordinary construction that it is not possible to describe it with a pen, particularly since it is like no other building in the world. It has towers and decoration and all the refinements which the human genius can conceive of. There are many smaller towers of similar style, in the same stone, which are gilded. The temple is surrounded by a moat, and access is by a single bridge, protected by two stone tigers so grand and fearsome as to strike terror into the visitor.

Other Portuguese missionaries were similarly awestruck by the scale of all they witnessed. In the words of Marcello de Ribadeneyra in the first account of Angkor in a Western language, published in 1601:

> We suppose that the founders of the kingdom of Siam came from the great city which is situated in the middle of a desert in the kingdom of Cambodia. There are the ruins of an ancient city there which some say was built by Alexander the Great or the Romans, it is amazing that no one lives there now, it is inhabited by ferocious animals, and the local people say it was built by foreigners.

Three years later, Gabriel de San Antonio described inscriptions that no one could read, and stone houses, courts, rooms and elevations, which appeared to be Roman. Father Antonio Dorta and Father Luys de Fonseca had spent many days there, he said, and they noted the fountains, canals and temples and the bridges supported by stone giants. 'There is a temple with five towers, called Angor.'

Many uninformed guesses were subsequently offered as to the nature of the monuments and their origins, virtually none of which gave credit to the Cambodian people. A common theme is that they could not possibly have been responsible for such splendour. An account published in Madrid in 1647 stated that 'A learned man supposed these to be the work of Trajan.'

The results of years of painstaking research have now replaced these early speculations. We now know that Angkor was the capital of a civilization, which in its prime, from AD 800 to 1400, commanded the rich lowlands of Cambodia and much of modern Thailand. Its god-kings lived in cities built to represent the mythical mountain home of the Hindu gods, surrounded by huge moats that symbolized the encircling oceans. We can gain a compelling image of life in the city of King Indravarman III from a remarkable contemporary account. In 1296, Zhou Daguan, a Chinese visitor, saw Angkor when it bustled with activity. He described a royal procession with King Indravarman holding *preah khan*, the sacred sword. In his own words:

> When the king goes out, troops are at the head of the escort; then come flags, banners and music. Palace women, numbering from three to five hundred, wearing flowered cloth, with flowers in their hair, hold candles in their hands, and form a troupe. Even in broad daylight, the candles are lighted. Then come other palace women, carrying lances and shields, the king's private guards, and carts drawn by goats and horses, all in gold, come next. Ministers and princes are mounted on elephants, and in front of them one can see, from afar, their innumerable red umbrellas. After them come the wives and concubines of the king, in palanquins, carriages, on horseback and on elephants. They have more than one hundred parasols, flecked with gold. Behind them comes the sovereign, standing on an elephant, holding his sacred sword in his hand. The elephant's tusks are encased in gold.

He visited the gilded palace and the towers of gold and bronze, and admired the 'tomb of Lu Pan', a monument we now call Angkor Wat. The lotus towers, the long galleries of bas-reliefs, the

3

surrounding walls and broad moat not only excite admiration, but provide an understanding of court rituals – even their conceptions of heaven and hell. Zhou Daguan also visited the Bayon, the great temple mausoleum of King Jayavarman VII, which lay at the centre of the city. Then as now, the reliefs carved in stone provide a rich insight into the daily life of the inhabitants: we can see men quietly playing chess, visit the interior of a Chinese merchant's house, or pass by a pavilion where midwives attend a woman in childbirth.

What was Angkor?

This book sets the supreme architectural achievement of the civilization of Angkor in its historic context. It begins deep in the prehistoric past, and explores Angkor from its earliest foundations, the stages that culminated in Angkor Wat, and beyond, to trace its decline and abandonment. What could have motivated the architects and labourers who toiled in the oppressive heat, hewing huge sandstone blocks and bringing them 30 kilometres to the northern shores of the Great Lake, the Tonle Sap, from the Kulen Hills? What mind conceived of a massive reservoir measuring 8 × 2.2 kilometres? Who carved the inscriptions, and what is their message? The first Portuguese missionaries could only guess, but after over a century of dedicated research, the inscriptions have been translated, the stones cleared and restored, the names of the kings and their dynasties returned from oblivion and some of the above questions answered.

Angkor is the name conventionally given to the cities and the associated monuments that lie between the Tonle Sap and the Kulen Hills. The word derives from the Sanskrit *nagara*, meaning 'holy city'. Viewed from the air, it is possible to detect the outlines of cities, reservoirs and temples, which reflect constant urban renewal. New temples continued to be built there over a period of at least seven centuries from about AD 700.

Illuminating an extinct civilization is a demanding and challenging endeavour, but also one with special rewards. This is

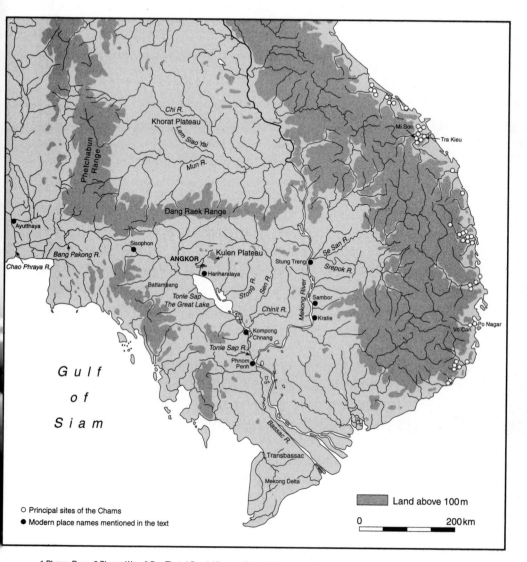

1 Phnom Rung, 2 Phnom Wan, 3 Ban That, 4 Preah Vihear, 5 Phimai, 6 Lopburi, 7 Phnom Sandak, 8 Yay Hom, 9 Phnom Bayang, 10 Wat Phu, 11 Wat Kok Po, 12 Banteay Chmar, 13 Baset

The location of places mentioned in the text.

particularly the case for the Western scholar where the civilization of Angkor is concerned, because the people, the religion, the environment, indeed virtually all aspects of its life and culture are alien. It means drawing on research in many fields, such as prehistoric archaeology, epigraphy, art history and the study of comparative religions, covering a span of 2000 years, which can be divided into four phases. Civilization at Angkor had its origins in the prehistoric Iron Age, which began about 500 BC. The second phase started in about AD 150, when the earliest state, often referred to as Funan after early Chinese reports, was forming in the Mekong Delta. This state declined due largely to changing trade patterns. It was superseded by the third phase which, from AD 550 to 800, saw several leaders competing for power in what may be called the core area of Angkor, the low-lying plains of central Cambodia from the delta to the Great Lake and up to the confluence of the Mekong and Mun rivers in north-east Thailand. This period is often called Chenla, again after the name used in Chinese documents. The fourth phase followed the establishment of a royal centre north of the Great Lake at Angkor.

Before describing this sequence, it is necessary to review certain key issues, which penetrate the fabric of the civilization of Angkor and allow for a deeper understanding of its history. These help to answer three questions: what is a state, how does it come into being, and how is it maintained?

The origins of states

Most anthropologists recognize that states evolve from chiefdoms, in which leaders dominate a social web where individuals are related by kinship. They usually involve a central settlement in which the chief resides, and one or two categories of smaller, dependent settlements. The chief is usually distinguished by symbols of status, and will often be accorded elaborate mortuary rites.

In a state, although kin ties remain, people are also identified by their class within a complex social network in which there are at least two endogamous groups, one comprising the ruling elite. The royal tier will usually be accorded a divine origin and the ability to communicate with the gods. There are four levels of settlement hierarchy from the capital down through provincial centres to villages. The king usually will live in a palace, and play an important role in rituals. His court absorbs surplus production from a much larger sustaining area than in a chiefdom, and high-ranking members of the court are recognized by special titles, offices and symbols of status. The regulation of labour and the appropriation of surplus production is essential in the support or maintenance of the administrative machinery for an enforceable legal system, an army, full-time priests and state temples.

Recent instances of state formation have stressed the importance of warfare, the control of power and trade, qualities of leadership and command of ritual. The eighteenth- and nineteenth-century history of the Yao people in Malawi illustrate these clearly. Although these people lived far from South-East Asia, the recorded course of their development is so similar to what we think might have occurred in the Mekong Delta that their experience will be briefly summarized here.

Traditionally, the Yao lived in inland villages dominated by women. A group of sisters, who defined their relationship through maternal ancestry, would appoint their oldest living brother as the village headman. Villages rarely exceeded fifty or sixty inhabitants, for this social system encouraged young aspiring leaders to leave and found their own settlement.

The situation changed radically as Arab traders began to explore the coast to the east. They sought ivory and slaves, and in return, supplied the Yao with beads, cloth and metal wire. Traditionally, the headman controlled trade, in which role he provided the blessing of the ancestors on traders when they left his village, often on hazardous journeys. He also had the right to distribute goods on their return. At the same time, the headman's prestige was measured by the size of his village, and the number of his followers. A demand for slaves engendered much tension among the Yao and their neighbours. Male slaves would be sent down to the coast to be sold. Female slaves could be kept by the chief as his own, thereby increasing his retinue. It is recorded that one chief, Mataka I Nyambi, owned 600 houses in eight villages, one house for each of his wives.

The transition from village headman to great chief was swift, happening in the space of half a life span. As the emerging chiefs expanded their domains and increased their power through trading for guns, so they adopted the exotic manners and customs of the Arab traders. This enhanced their prestige in the eyes of their followers. Some accepted Islam, and changed their names: chief Monjesa became Zuraf. Sultan Che Mataka had exotic trees planted, and changed the name of his capital to Mwembe, meaning 'tree of the coast'. Chief Makanjila had his palace built in the Arab style. They began to use Arab writing to keep their records. As towns developed from villages, it became necessary to grow more food, and irrigation water was brought to their fields. When Sultan Che Mataka died, he was accompanied in his grave by thirty boys and girls, dressed in special cloth. They were armed with guns and powder horns, and accompanied by offerings of salt and beads.

Similar changes in behaviour in South-East Asia should leave archaeological traces, or alert us to the significance of the words contained in inscriptions and eye-witness accounts. The first pre-requisite in seeking the origins of Angkor is to define a period when there were competing chiefdoms. Archaeological signatures of this are a dense distribution of large settlements, rich burials of the elite and the material remains of warfare. Evidence for palaces, records of taxation, the control of labour to construct public buildings and agricultural improvements, as well as the adoption of an exotic Indian writing system and language, or of the appointment of followers over dependent settlements, signal the emergence of a state. Once formed, a state had to maintain itself. Many archaic states had brief lives, often characterized by construction activity and territorial expansion, followed by contraction or subjugation by rivals.

Influence from India

One of the most contentious issues in the historiography of the Angkorian state is the depth of its debt to Indian religion and political philosophy. Some early interpretations of the state of Angkor stressed the seminal role of India in its formation and nature. Beguiled by the ubiquitous imagery of Shiva and Vishnu, central gods in the Indian pantheon, and the use of Sanskrit, the priestly language of Hinduism, Indianization was put forward as a possible process to explain the origins of Angkor. There is no doubt that the people of South-East Asia exchanged goods and ideas with India from at least 350 BC. But it will be seen that the local rulers chose to adopt Indic gods and language to their own advantage rather than having Hinduism imposed upon them from outside. Indeed, for most of its history, the rulers of Angkor professed devotion to ancestral divinities and Hindu gods rather than to the Buddha. Therefore, an understanding of Hindu religion, ritual and the importance of merit is necessary to clarify the content of many Angkorian inscriptions.

The Hindu sacred texts, or *puranas*, describe the universe as being centred upon Mount Meru, ringed by a series of concentric circles. The first is known as *jambudvipa*, the land of the rose apple tree, beyond which lies the salt-water ocean, and so through various realms until one reaches outer darkness. There are also seven layers below the surface, under which lie the realms of hell. The social anthropologist Stanley Tambiah has suggested, on the basis of the Thai states of Sukhothai and Ayutthaya, that the capital represented Mount Meru, home of the Hindu gods, ringed by mountains (walls) and oceans (moats). The cosmos is inhabited by many kinds of beings, including divine nymphs or *apsaras*, and mythical snakes, the *nagas*. The king was the divine intermediary between the world of gods and people. Reincarnation is a central feature of Hinduism, and accumulating merit through a worthy lifestyle, or making offerings to the gods, determines one's place in any of these realms after death.

The myriad gods of the Hindu pantheon are worshipped

9

through the medium of the *puja*, or offering. Such merit-making centres on a gift of food, fruit, flowers, clothing or, in rare cases, meat or symbolic blood, which increases the donor's store of merit. The image of the deity is awakened, bathed, rubbed with sesame oil and provided with fresh clothing. It is entertained throughout the day by musicians and dancers, praised and worshipped. Lamps are burnt, tapers rotated before the god, and the priest will bring his burning lamp to devotees for them to place their hands over it and receive blessings and merit. In the evening, the god is feasted, undressed and retired for the night.

Temples are not only immensely rich but important spiritual and economic institutions. They traditionally derived wealth from land assigned them by the king, from meritorious donations and fees for religious services. Within their walls, temples are virtually self-contained communities with their own bathing tanks, offices, dispensaries, schoolrooms and even banks.

Merit can also be accrued by making pilgrimages to the great temples and holy locations, such as the source of the Ganges. Death is marked by *pinda*, offerings of rice to the dead over a period of ten days, to reconstruct the body so that it can leave its temporary abode in the land of ghosts and join the realm of the ancestors. Astrological observations are a vital part of determining the course of one's life. The use of a twelve-year cycle is widespread in India and South-East Asia. In India, the cycle is determined by the motions of Jupiter; in South-East Asia it is characterized by twelve animal names of remote origin. The cycle remains particularly auspicious today as in the past.

There are key pan-Hindu gods and countless regional deities. This is essential to understanding why there are so many named gods in Angkorian inscriptions, many being of local or ancestral origin. Vishnu is the supreme god, who descends to the world of mortals in many guises. One of these, a turtle, was very popular at Angkor, as Vishnu represented thus supported the world during the churning of the ocean of milk to obtain the elixir of immortality. Shiva is a second major god, who became popular at Angkor. He may be represented in many forms, the most popular being as a *linga*, an erect stone phallus within a *yoni*, or vulva, symbolic of the union of Shiva with *sakti*, his dynamic energy.

The manifestation of royal and divine essences in the form of the royal *linga* at Angkor reflects the way in which esoteric ritual could augment status. It is also vital to understand that the gifting of food, clothing and oil to a temple was a way for the donor to accumulate merit and ensure a harmonious reincarnation. Such rituals, in theory, also materially helped bind the provinces to the palace and the state temple, the representation of Mount Meru. While this principle was doubtless acknowledged by all, the civilization of Angkor was still fractured by conflict and instability. In the central court, there was the problem of rights of succession. There was no tradition of primogeniture, and in a situation where kings were polygamous, descent through the female line remained significant. Thus the potential for factionalism and dissension was ever present. This was exacerbated where royal claimants, or provincial aristocrats, could build up regional loyalties and power bases.

The importance of rice

Another contentious and most important issue is the organization of agriculture. States are fuelled by the energy supplied by agricultural surpluses. In Cambodia, this means the cultivation of rice and, as we will see, the inscriptions contain countless allusions to the ownership of rice fields and the supply of grain to the regional and central temples.

There are two opposed schools of thought on how agriculture was organized. One proposes that the massive reservoirs at Angkor were controlled by the king, and were used to irrigate rice fields for three or even four harvests a year. The other denies any state-directed irrigation and argues in favour of the dispersed rain-fed system seen today, supplemented by various other harvesting methods that do not call on irrigation controls. Advocates of the former see royally inspired irrigation not only as a key factor in the rise of the civilization of Angkor, but in its collapse as the network failed. The latter viewpoint sees the reservoirs as playing a symbolic role by representing the oceans surrounding the home of the gods.

None of these variables exists in isolation. By weaving together the many strands that made up the civilization of Angkor, and seeking a pattern to the changes that took place over two millennia, it will be possible to understand why such monuments as Angkor Wat were built and what they meant to those who saw the golden towers in their heyday. We can also seek answers to why this holy city had been abandoned and consumed by the jungle when the first Portuguese missionaries passed in wonder through its great stone gates.

CHAPTER 2

THE PREHISTORIC PERIOD
IN SOUTH-EAST ASIA:
2300 BC–AD 400

Most general surveys of South-East Asian states begin with a ritual nod towards the late prehistoric period. Until recently, this period has been a grey area. Our understanding of communities there and their occupants owed more to the imagination of historians than to proper archaeological enquiry. Georges Cœdès, the influential French authority, described them as a backward people, who absorbed the influence of Indian traders and Brahmans. The Russian historian Sedov wrote: 'The beginning of the new era finds the Khmer tribes at the stage of the Iron Age culture. The population, sparse as it was, is made up of tribal clan communities with strong internal kinship ties and living relatively isolated from each other, though mutually at peace' (Sedov, 1978: 111).

Recent excavations have shown beyond doubt that almost every word of this is either unproven or wrong. The prehistoric societies of South-East Asia were vigorous and powerful. They were engaged in distant maritime exchange, and their leaders organized large-scale water control measures. They maintained specialized bronze and iron workshops, and were recognized in death with rich burials, which would include gold and silver jewellery and hundreds of bronze ornaments. A proper understanding of these societies is essential in tracing the origins of the civilization of Angkor. This must begin with an appreciation of the importance to them of rice cultivation.

Rice cultivation: its origins and importance

Until the arrival of the first rice farmers about 4300 years ago, hunter-gatherers lived in the forested uplands and along the coast of South-East Asia. Traces of the former are seen in rock shelters where thin occupation layers attest to their occupation. The latter had the advantage of access to rich coastal resources, and their large and permanent settlements reveal considerable wealth and social complexity. Being dependent upon nature's bounty, however, placed these communities in a cultural cul-de-sac. The pathway to civilization required the energy provided by rice agriculture. Indeed, the domestication of rice represents one of the most profound changes in the human past of South-East Asia. This reflects the adaptability of this marsh grass, its nutritional value especially when it is consumed with fish, the degree to which the landscape can be modified to expand its production, and the relative ease with which it can be stored. Rice is the solid rock upon which South-East Asian civilizations were founded.

The landscape that nurtured the civilization of Angkor is low-lying, flat and often flooded. The Mekong River forms a north–south thoroughfare, while east–west movement is facilitated by the Tonle Sap River and the Great Lake. Many tributaries feed these rivers and lake, and their flood plains are dotted with Angkorian sites. Occasionally, one sees isolated hills or, in the case of the Kulen plateau, a substantial upland. Further north, the Dang Raek escarpment divides Cambodia from Thailand, although it is easily crossed and leads on to the Mun River basin.

This land is dominated by the monsoon. The rains fall from May to October. The Mekong River, fed by the monsoon and the spring melt of snow in the Himalayas, bursts its banks and flood waters sweep across the flood plain and delta. At Phnom Penh, where the Mekong meets the Tonle Sap River, the waters reverse their normal flow, backing up and swelling the Great Lake. But even this safety valve cannot prevent floods across the lower course of the Mekong and its delta. The dry season follows from November to May. Floods recede, and away from the flood plains, the exposed soil in the rice fields hardens and cracks. Cool in January, the weather becomes increasingly hot, until by April, it is hardly bearable. Then the rains break, and heavy thunderstorms track across the parched lowlands bringing relief from the heat, softening the soil and again filling the rivers to overflowing.

This pattern has encouraged several different methods of growing rice, depending on the local water regime. In the deeply flooded delta and flood plains of the Mekong and the Great Lake, it is not possible to grow rice during the rainy season, but flood water is retained in natural or artificial reservoirs in this period. Then in January, as the waters recede, the rice is planted out and sustained by water distributed from the reservoirs. In some cases, the rice is grown within the wet basins or reservoirs themselves. But on higher ground away from the flood plains, rainwater is retained in small fields by the construction of low bunds or walls of soil. Surveying these areas from the surrounding hills during the rainy season, one sees an unending carpet of emerald green, for rice is by nature an aquatic plant, which will grow on poor soils, provided that plentiful water brings the nitrogen-fixing algae that sustain growth.

These are two of the major methods for growing rice today, but we have surprisingly little information on how the people of Angkor grew their rice. Inscriptions mention rice field workers, but do not describe their seasonal round. The bas-reliefs of Angkor include fishing scenes and warfare, but not agricultural activities. Indeed, the purpose of the huge reservoirs at Angkor, and of the canals that criss-cross the Mekong Delta, remain controversial.

Tracing the transition from hunting and gathering to a rice-based economy, therefore, is an essential way station in understanding the origins of civilization. The state of Angkor incorporated many classes. There was the royal court with its army of administrators; below this, priests, officiants in the central and regional temples; doctors, architects and generals. Without a surplus of rice, this edifice would have collapsed. It is, therefore, hardly surprising to find that many surviving

Angkorian texts are concerned with land boundaries and the provision of taxation in the form of surplus agricultural production.

Where did the vital transition to rice domestication occur? According to recent research in the Yangzi Valley, it took place there about 6500 BC. Pengtoushan is a well-known early site, where a village cemetery, houses, pottery vessels and skilfully manufactured stone ornaments all signal major cultural changes. By 5000 BC, rice farmers had reached the mouth of the Yangzi River. In southern China, we encounter rice farmers at Shixia by 2800 BC, their material culture showing many parallels with their relatives further north. Similarly in Vietnam, the first rice farmers settled the Red River valley by the end of the third millennium BC. There is a corresponding pattern in the valley of the Mekong River. Neolithic sites involving rice cultivation and domestic cattle, pigs and dogs are rare, and date from about 2200 BC. Samrong Sen, a site in the heartland of the later Angkor civilization, belongs to this tradition. These early intrusive farmers probably spoke ancestral Khmer (the language of Cambodia), Vietnamese and Mon, which is still spoken in isolated parts of Thailand. These languages are related, and are thought to have a common origin in the groups of expansive early rice farmers.

The slowness of their advance into South-East Asia during the third millennium BC explains why civilization there developed so late. As they reached Cambodia, the Shang state was already forming in China. It takes time for rice farmers to explore, settle and proliferate, particularly when confronting trackless forests, as in South-East Asia. Neolithic sites were few, scattered and small, and probably harboured fewer than 100 individuals. The people grew rice and maintained domestic cattle, pigs and dogs, but also turned to local resources, such as fish, shellfish, deer and wild cattle. Human remains found in the area reflect a nutritious diet, but we know virtually nothing about the life expectancy, infant mortality, or health of the population, due to the absence of any large-scale excavation. Also, the Neolithic period was short, perhaps lasting no longer than eight centuries in Cambodia and adjacent parts of Thailand, and substantial areas may have had a very low population density, if indeed there were any settlements at all.

The Bronze Age

Many scholars now agree that the knowledge of how to smelt copper and tin ores, and then combine them to cast bronzes, came to China from the Near East. By 1500 BC, the Bronze Age in China was already well established in the Shang civilization. Some Shang jades and bronzes were traded in southern China and Vietnam, and this seems the most likely source for the beginnings of the Bronze Age in South-East Asia. From Hong Kong to the Chindwin Valley in Burma, we find Bronze Age settlements, dated within the period 1500–500 BC.

Copper ore is found in the uplands of South-East Asia, and Malaysia and Thailand contain one of the world's major sources of tin ore. Excavations over the past thirty years have disclosed the principal features of the South-East Asian Bronze Age. There appears to have been a smooth transition from the Neolithic into the early Bronze Age. Two mining complexes (one at Phu Lon in north-east Thailand, near the Mekong River, and another, a large complex of mines and associated processing sites, in central Thailand) have revealed that the copper ore was extracted by following the seams into the mountainside, and that it was then concentrated and smelted in small bowl furnaces near the mines. Much of the copper was cast into circular ingots, destined for trade, but there does not appear to have been an organizing elite with a subservient workforce. Rather, the mines were probably worked during the dry season by the members of local rice farming communities. At the site of Non Pa Wai in central Thailand, the cemetery of such a group has been uncovered. People were buried with their ceramic casting moulds and bronzes, but no single individual stands out as being unusually wealthy. A second cemetery at Nil Kham Haeng is later, and burials there extended into the Iron Age.

The ingots reached their final destination in small villages often located hundreds of kilometres from the mines. Ban Na Di in north-east Thailand is one of several such sites where excavations have revealed not only cemeteries but bronze-casting furnaces, crucibles and moulds, providing a fount of information on the people, their social order, economy and technology. The dead were buried in at least two orderly clusters, one of which contained richer graves with more exotic offerings, such as bangles made of bronze, marine shell, marble and slate. One child had been buried under a crocodile-skin shroud; a woman nearby wore a large pendant fashioned from the skull of a crocodile. This wealthier part of the site also included a number of clay figurines representing cattle, deer, people and an elephant. All the individuals were well fed and had a robust bone structure, but life expectancy remained low, with many infant deaths and few adults surviving beyond the age of thirty-five.

Other excavated sites present variations on the same theme. At a cemetery in Nong Nor in central Thailand, one group of graves was rather more wealthy than the others. Here, we find grave goods of bronze, in the form of bangles, but also of unalloyed tin and copper. Exotic ornaments were made from jade, talc, serpentine, carnelian and marble. Bronze Age graves at Ban Lum Khao in the upper Mun Valley contain marble and shell bangles, and an abundance of attractive red pottery vessels. Further north again, at Non Nok Tha, many pottery vessels were found, along with stone moulds for casting socketed axes, and some bronze bangles and axes.

Sites remained small, with none exceeding a few hectares. There is no evidence for any form of authority beyond each village, and the picture is one of scattered settlements, which communicated by the exchange of goods and probably marriage partners. The people grew rice and maintained domestic stock; lived in communities where their ancestors' graves accumulated over many generations; and tuned their lives to the rhythm of the monsoon.

The Iron Age

With the coming of the Iron Age, we approach the origins of civilization. Iron was being smelted in this area by about 500 BC, and its impact was direct and potent. Iron ore is abundant and widespread, but iron itself is more difficult to obtain than copper or tin, because it requires a much higher smelting temperature. We do not know how the knowledge of ironworking reached South-East Asia. It may have been a local innovation, but the possible spread of expertise from China or India cannot be ruled out.

The nature of Iron Age culture on the eve of civilization has been a vital but previously missing part of the jigsaw. The best evidence for Iron Age society in the area of the later civilization of Angkor comes from north-east Thailand. By this time there were many more settlement sites, and they were much bigger. Non Muang Kao (Mound of the Ancient City) covered about 50 hectares, with a population probably in the region of 2500. Excavations at the nearby site of Noen U-Loke in 1997–8 have revealed occupation beginning in the late Bronze Age (600 BC) and ending by about AD 400, the period of transition to early states. The site is one of many in the Mun Valley and the plains surrounding the Great Lake in Cambodia, which are ringed by banks and moats. This Iron Age society is defined not only by the evidence of its burials, but also by the nature of its technology, the economic basis of its communities, the extent to which its trade in exotic goods quickened relative to the Bronze Age, and the nature of its surrounding earthworks and moats.

The creation of the moats has now been dated to the late Iron Age (AD 100–500). While their functions remain elusive, the extent of the earthworks reveals that it was a major undertaking, no doubt helped by the availability of iron spades. Many sites were occupied: Ban Don Phlong, Non Yang, Ban Takhong and Ban Krabuang Nok have all been investigated by excavation and dated to the Iron Age. At Non Dua, prehistoric layers lie beneath an Angkorian temple. Similar sites extend south of the Dang Raek range into Cambodia, Lovea being one such settlement lying only a few kilometres north-west of Angkor itself.

In the low-lying, watery habitat of the Mun Valley, the site of Noen U-Loke expanded over an area of 12 hectares. Iron was present early in the sequence. In its cemetery, a woman was found wearing an iron torc or neck ring and three iron bangles, whilst a man was interred with an iron hoe and a large socketed iron spear. Around his neck were bronze torcs and a necklace made of tigers' teeth. His earlobes had been cut and filled with shell discs, and he wore bronze bangles. One of his pottery vessels contained fish skeletons, and alongside it lay two bronze spears.

These early burials were few and dispersed, but later phases revealed distinct clusters of interments, when the energy that these people expended on graves increased dramatically. Some of the dead were placed in graves filled with burnt rice, while certain graves were also lined and capped with clay coffins. Each cluster included the remains of men, women, children and infants laid out in close proximity. In some cases, it proved possible to trace singular characteristics associated with certain groups. One contained almost all the carnelian jewellery and a great deal of rice. Another held many spindle whorls and a third, most of the clay-lined coffins. There was also an outstandingly rich adult in three of the clusters. One included a man wearing three bronze belts with clips to fasten them in place, about seventy-five bronze bangles on each arm, numerous bronze finger and toe rings, glass beads round the neck and ankles, and silver ear coils bearing gold leaf. Another man wore four bronze belts, large bronze ear discs, and many bronze bangles, ear and toe rings. The third, a woman, was found with bronze bangles, bronze and silver finger and toe rings, and a necklace of gold and agate beads. All were accompanied by superb black pottery vessels and iron knives, one of which bore traces of clothing. These rich burials suggest not only the high standing of some individuals, but also the possibility of social ranking. This trend developed as labour was organized to ring sites with banks and moats. There is also evidence for fighting. The discovery of iron spears and arrowheads including one found lodged in the spine of a man lying prone, support this conjecture.

Whilst copper and tin had to be imported from the mines of central Thailand, iron was locally smelted and forged. The iron-workers applied their skills not only to ornaments and weaponry, but also to agriculture. One grave contained a winged and socket-ed iron spade, still covered in rice. In the final mortuary phase, iron sickles were found in some of the burials and socketed hoes were relatively common. It is also possible that the artisans at Noen U-Loke had mastered glass manufacture. Little evidence has been found, however, for a ceramic industry, and it may well be that the eggshell-thin vessels accompanying the dead were imported from the workshops of full-time specialists.

The excavations at Noen U-Loke suggest a vigorous and innova-tive community, adept at manufacture and the expansion of agri-cultural production. It was, however, only one of many such settlements in the Mun Valley, and there are still more further south towards Angkor itself. Wherever excavations have been undertaken, a similar pattern of social change has been found. We see the same clay-lined coffins as at Noen U-Loke, and a parallel range of exotic grave goods, including carnelian, agate, gold and glass. Iron-smelting furnaces and salt-making facilities abound. Iron weapons and tools proliferated, and copper and tin production must have escalated, given the huge increase in the number of bronze ornaments encountered. In some river valleys, the moated sites are so crowded as to be virtually within hailing distance of each other.

When looking beyond the Mun Valley and northern Cambodia, we find similar evidence of increasing social complexity. Ban Don Ta Phet in central Thailand is critical in understanding the bur-geoning trade links with India by the fourth century BC. Burials there were accompanied by decorated bronze bowls, etched car-nelian beads and a leaping lion in carnelian, all of which come from India. Other ornaments from this and related sites reveal how Iron Age communities participated in a maritime trade network, which linked them to the islands of South-East Asia, New Guinea, the Philippines and beyond, to China and India.

This pattern is characteristic of other parts of South-East Asia.

On the coast of central Vietnam, there are rich urnfields, where lidded jars contain human ashes with exotic ornaments, iron tools and weapons. As history dawned, these people are known to us as the civilization of Champa. From Yunnan to Guangdong in southern China, and in the delta of the Red River, rich and warlike chiefdoms emerged as the first millennium BC drew to a close. Their internal development, however, ended abruptly when they were incorporated into the Han empire of China.

Far from being cowering natives or poor savages, the Iron Age ancestors of Angkor lived in large communities in which some individuals, both men and women, were interred with opulent grave goods and much ritual. Iron was employed not only to increase agricultural efficiency but to forge weapons of war. Salt processing reached an industrial scale; specialists were able to produce for their leaders outstanding ceramic vessels and ornaments of bronze, glass, gold, silver, carnelian and agate. There was increased competition and conflict, as skilled and intrepid navigators engaged in international trade. Iron Age chiefdoms were now poised for the transition to the state.

CHAPTER 3

THE EARLIEST CIVILIZATION IN SOUTH-EAST ASIA: AD 150–550

The Mekong River lances through the heart of South-East Asia. It has from time immemorial provided passage for the movement of people, goods and ideas, including the earliest intrusive farmers and the trade in copper and tin. During the Iron Age, it was used to transport south large ceremonial bronze drums from Yunnan and Vietnam. In 1644, the Dutch merchant Geritt van Wuystoff travelled up the Mekong River to Vientiane in Laos, and nineteenth-century French explorers followed its route from the delta to Yunnan. Its vital importance during both the formation and the apogee of the civilization of Angkor is hard to overestimate.

At Phnom Penh, the river divides first into the Mekong and Bassac branches, then into a myriad of channels as it meets the South China Sea. Here, it drops its burden of sediment to form the flat, hot delta. The axis formed by the river and coast provided outstanding opportunities for trade. Once again, Sedov misunderstood the prehistoric situation when he wrote: 'Indian immigrants, colonists and traders brought with them their own ideas of government, customs and fashions, and religious symbolism. They acquainted the aborigines with various new techniques, including methods of land reclamation, and with handicrafts and the art of war' (Sedov, 1978: 111).

We now know that by 380 BC, Iron Age communities in central Thailand had already opened trade relations with India. The Sa Huynh people of coastal Vietnam, who probably arrived there from the islands to the south by about 500 BC, were highly competent navigators. Boats in South-East Asia from the first millennium AD attest to a long tradition of skilled construction, in which the main planks are stitched together and lugs and lashing are added to give strength. At Pontian in Malaysia, such vessels have been radiocarbon-dated to between the third and the fifth centuries AD. A further example, dating two centuries later, has been unearthed at Palembang. According to early Chinese reports, some South-East Asian ocean-going vessels dating to the first century AD were up to 50 metres in length and weighed over 600 tons. This vigorous tradition of Iron Age maritime trade received added stimulus as South-East Asia provided key links in a chain of trading ports connecting the empires of East and West.

Funan, the delta state

Chinese dynastic records include a remarkable report from Kang Tai and Zhu Ying, emissaries of the Wu emperor. They travelled to South-East Asia in the third century AD, probably to investigate the possibility of opening a maritime silk route between China and Rome. Their report described a polity on the Mekong Delta, which they named Funan, where they found settlements ringed by wooden palisades, palaces, houses raised on stilts and rice cultivation. The Chinese visitors noted that ornaments were engraved, and that there was a tax on gold, silver, pearls and perfumes. Writing was known, in a script resembling that of the Hu (who were in turn influenced from India), and there was a legal system involving the trial of suspects by ordeal.

The History of the Liang Dynasty of China, which dates from the first half of the sixth century AD, may have employed Kang Tai's report as one of its sources. It relates how a leader named Fan Shih Man employed his soldiers to subdue neighbouring rulers. He also attacked other settlements by sea, and put his sons in charge of the conquered chiefdoms. He assumed the title 'Great King' and his capital was located inland, 500 *li* from the sea. Since the length of a *li* varied with time, estimating the distance is not easy but the actual capital was probably the site of Angkor Borei.

There were clearly disputes over kingship. Following the death of the king, a nephew seized power by force, but he in turn was deposed by a younger son of Fan Shih Man. Another military leader in yet another coup then seized power. Rulers of Funan sent at least twenty-five missions to China between AD 226 and 649, bearing gifts of gold, silver, tin and copper, valued kingfisher plumage, unusual animals such as elephant and rhinoceros, as well as ivory, turtles and gharuwood. Most of these items would have had to be obtained from the communities living beyond the confines of the delta, up the course of the Mekong River.

Such trade contacts would have accelerated the emergence of social elites, the very people able to organize commercial trading transactions. Such a trend not only sees the availability of a novel range of trading goods, but also stimulates local production to provide exports. Moreover, South-East Asian mariners would have experienced unfamiliar societies, ideas, technologies and languages. New opportunities for advancement also engendered rivalry and competition, thereby creating conflict and social change.

Oc Eo, a trading port

Kang Tai's description of cities, kings and palaces requires archaeological verification. Aerial photographs taken over the Mekong Delta in the 1920s revealed a network of ancient canals, one of which bisected the walls of an ancient city, 450 hectares in extent. On the ground, the French archaeologist Louis Malleret was able to find its walls and moats. Branching canals formed a regular pattern inside the perimeter, some enclosing rectangular structures, one of which was known as Oc Eo. This name was given by Malleret to the whole site. Could this city have been visited by the Chinese emissaries? Excavations began on 10

February 1944, and remarkably, Malleret discovered archaeological evidence for many of the activities described by Kang Tai eighteen centuries previously. In Area B, as he termed it, he found the remains of bricks, tiles, glass beads and pottery vessels at a depth of about a metre. Area D revealed the remains of a jewellery workshop, including fragments of gold, copper and bivalve moulds for casting tin ornaments. He encountered human bones in Area Q, but their layout could not be recognized, because they were covered by a layer of watery sand. But it was ascertained that there were two phases of cultural deposits, one 2 metres deep at this point. The waterlogged substrate had also preserved wooden posts, which would have raised buildings above the flood waters.

He then excavated one of the central mounds, revealing brick foundations and walls associated with ceramic figures of a lion, a unicorn-like animal and a monster. One ceramic tile was embellished with a cobra. The bricks were also decorated with geometric designs in low relief. He was left to speculate on the function of these constructions. Could they have been temple shrines, or mortuary structures? The decorated tiles, bricks and moulded animals suggested a religious or ritual function, a possibility supported by the recovery of a stone *linga*.

Malleret had located a critical site for understanding early trends to social complexity in South-East Asia. Its area exceeded by far that of any earlier settlement. The use of brick for large structures was also an innovation. There was a domestic element too, in the form of house foundations, pottery fragments, the remains of turtles, fish and the bones of domestic cattle and pigs. Oc Eo also harboured specialists in the manufacture of jewellery, for Malleret recovered their bronze awls and hammers. A mass of gold leaf and partially finished items indicated the local working of this metal, one of the end products being small gold plaques engraved or decorated by the repoussé technique. One woman is seen seated cross-legged, playing on a harp. A second gold plaque bears the image of a woman standing in a most graceful posture, with one arm close to her body, a lotus flower beside her head.

She wears an elaborate hairstyle, and an elegant loose-fitting skirt.

The local goldsmiths were probably also acquainted with Roman coinage. Malleret has published two examples, which were probably bought from local looters. One represents the emperor Antoninus Pius, dated to about AD 152, and has been modified into a pendant. A second, from the reign of the emperor Marcus Aurelius, appears to be a copy, for the reverse side is blank. Malleret has suggested that it was cast in a mould made as a negative of the original and destined to be worn as a pendant. A local coinage developed, with motifs including the sun and shellfish. It did not survive the life of Funan, however.

Malleret found convincing evidence, in the form of unfinished ornaments, for lapidaries at Oc Eo. The range of precious and semi-precious stones suggests considerable trading commerce, for the delta has few local resources. Carnelian, agate, amethyst, beryl, sapphires, zircon, quartz, diamonds, rubies, olivine, jade and the minerals malachite and magnetite were all employed in the manufacture of jewellery. Specialists also fashioned inscribed seals from carnelian, local manufacture again being indicated by the presence of unfinished examples. One bears the Sanskrit word *jaya*, or victory, inscribed in the Indian Brahmi script. Another has a personal name, a third the word 'attention'. Individuals are also depicted. A woman is seen, seated in front of a vessel from which flames emerge. It is tantalizingly difficult to determine whether this represents a ritual or a domestic activity. Another specimen shows a bearded Roman, of undoubted Mediterranean origin. Others were decorated with cattle, pigs, a dog and a lion. Roman coinage and other goods obtained from afar by trade denote that Oc Eo was occupied when Kang Tai visited Funan.

Despite so many important discoveries, much still remained to be done when wars brought research to a halt. Recently, Pierre-Yves Manguin and Vo Si Khai have returned to Oc Eo and the many sites scattered at the foot of the Ba The hill nearby. Their research programme is designed to investigate the wide range of sites on the plain below Ba The, including the moats, canals and walls, to obtain a solid dating framework for the critical centuries during which the sites were occupied and to illuminate the major stages of cultural development there. Early results at Linh Son and Go Cay Thi indicate the elements of the basic cultural sequence. There were settlements with houses raised on piles during the first century or two of the Christian era, representing essentially the late prehistoric occupation of the delta. There followed a period, between the fifth and the seventh centuries, when brick structures were erected. The moats, canals and walls might belong to this period, but remain to be dated. After a period of abandonment, the site was reoccupied during the early Angkorian period in the ninth and tenth centuries.

Angkor Borei

Kang Tai and Zhu Ying also described an inland capital. A canal linked Oc Eo with Angkor Borei, a walled city covering about 300 hectares, 90 kilometres to the north on the margin of the delta. Miriam Stark has recently commenced serious archaeological research there, concentrating initially on preparing a plan of the site with its visible surface monuments, then documenting the cultural sequence and establishing the chronology. Vital new information is now becoming available. Test squares have encountered over 5 metres of cultural build-up. The basal radio-carbon dates, when linked with the typology of the early bur- nished and incised pottery, show that Angkor Borei was occupied by at least the fourth century BC. An Iron Age cemetery contain- ing inhumation graves has been identified at the base of the sequence. There followed a series of habitation remains character- ized by a thin orange pottery, which appears to date between the first century BC and the sixth century AD. There is also some evi- dence of occupation of the site during the period of Angkor (AD 800–1430). In this context, dating the encircling walls and moats is a major objective. Might they have been begun in the period of Funan, the delta state, or are they some centuries later? The energy required in their construction may be gauged by the fact that in an exposed portion, the wall is 2.4 metres wide and 4.5 metres high, while the moats are 22 metres in width. Many mounds lie within the walls, one of which revealed a rectangular brick structure at least 19 × 20 metres in extent, the top of which bore many circular post holes. It might be that the brick base supported a wooden building. One of the temples has recently furnished a stone sculpture of Vishnu, dated, on stylistic grounds, to the seventh century AD.

There are also numerous rectangular water tanks or ponds; the Eastern Baray, or reservoir, covers an area of about 200 × 100 metres. The long dry season makes water conservation a necessary component of urban life. Even during the prehistoric Iron Age, settlements were ringed by banks to retain water. A *baray* follows the same principle, with raised rectangular embankments. Although the function of the *barays* is not known in detail and may have changed over time, domestic needs were doubtless prominent.

Recent archaeological research in the delta

Post-war research in the delta has added considerably to our knowledge of the range of monuments and the chronology of this early civilization. Trading communities were already established towards the end of the first millennium BC, for at Go Hang, a range of glass, agate and carnelian beads matching those from Noen U-Loke has been recovered, with a radiocarbon date of 54 BC–AD 130. The archaeological record then reveals a major transformation. The site of Nen Chua, for example, incorporates a rectangular structure in stone and brick 25.7 × 16.3 metres in extent, with what look like two internal chambers. The presence of a *linga* and gold ornaments suggests that it had a religious focus. This same site has provided evidence for a radical change in mortuary rituals, compared with the age-old prehistoric tradition of inhumation. Small brick-lined chambers dug up to 2.5 metres into the ground received cremated remains, associated with

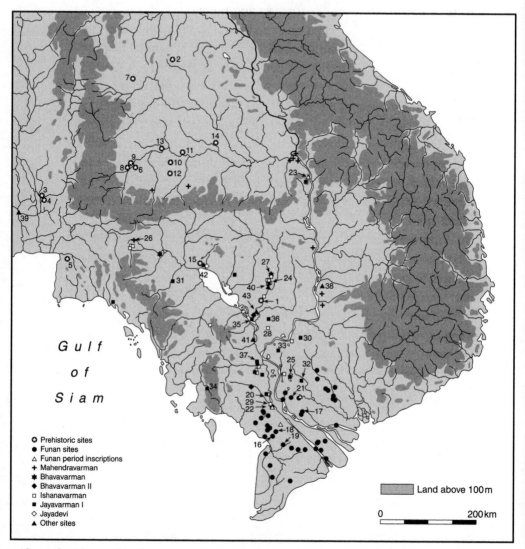

Key (map legend):
○ Prehistoric sites
● Funan sites
△ Funan period inscriptions
+ Mahendravarman
✳ Bhavavarman
◆ Bhavavarman II
□ Ishanavarman
■ Jayavarman I
◇ Jayadevi
▲ Other sites

Land above 100 m

0   200 km

1 Samrong Sen, 2 Ban Na Di, 3 Non Pa Wai, 4 Nil Kham Haeng, 5 Nong Nor, 6 Ban Lum Khao, 7 Non Nok Tha, 8 Non Muang Kao,
9 Noen U-Loke, 10 Ban Don Phlong, 11 Non Yang, 12 Ban Takhong, 13 Ban Krabuang Nok, 14 Non Dua, 15 Lovea, 16 Nen Chua,
17 Go Thap, 18 Oc Eo, 19 Da Noi, 20 Angkor Borei, Phnom Da, 21 Go Hang, 22 Nak Ta Dambang Dek, 23 Wat Phu,
24 Sambor Prei Kuk, Ishanapura, 25 Wat Kdei Ang, Wat Chakret, 26 Aranyaprathet, 27 Roban Romas, 28 Kuk Prah Kot, 29 Wat Po,
30 Tuol Kok Prah, 31 Wat Po Val, 32 Wat Prei Val, 33 Tuol Prah That, 34 Prah Kuha Luon, 35 Tan Kran, 36 Wat Baray, 37 Tuol Nak Ta Bak Ka,
38 Wat Tasar Moroy, 39 Ayutthaya, 40 Wat En Khna, 41 Lonvek, 42 Wat Khnat, 43 Ampil Rolum

The distribution of sites relating to the early Delta or Funan state and of the early
Kingdoms.

rectangular or oval gold leaves decorated with human forms with raised right hands. One such image appears to have four arms and might represent Harihara, the combined image of Shiva and Vishnu. The radiocarbon dates from this site suggest occupation within the period AD 450–650.

Eight similar graves have been unearthed at Go Thap, well known for a sixth-century Sanskrit inscription. An early pre-historic settlement preceded a 1-hectare burial mound in which graves were enclosed by a brick wall 7 × 10 metres in extent. Brick-lined pits within contained human ashes and mortuary offerings. These comprised 322 gold leaves, 5 gold discs, 3 gold rings, a gold flower, 8 precious stones and 7 pieces of glass. The gold leaves were decorated with deities, turtles representing Vishnu and his mount, the eagle Garuda, water buffaloes, ele-phants, snakes, conch shells, the sun, plants and a house on piles, many of these symbols relating to Hindu gods. The excavator described one as a buffalo with a stick in its mouth, but the stick might equally represent the cord often seen threaded through a buffalo's nose to guide it when ploughing. A second scene depicts a man holding what might be a harness of some sort, leading to two sets of symbolic horns. Again, this might indicate the adop-tion of the plough. Two radiocarbon dates indicate that the cemetery falls within the period AD 400–600.

At Go Cay Trom, excavations have unearthed the brick founda-tions for a monument 30 metres square associated with a *linga* that the excavators assigned to the fifth to sixth centuries AD. Further gold leaves have been found at the brick temple of Go Xoai, one of which has a Sanskrit inscription dated to the fifth century AD. The two rectangular brick buildings from Cay Gao are linked to a single radiocarbon date of AD 240–440, but more dating is necessary before such an early context can be accepted. Apart from the recovery of burial and religious sites, several wooden images of deities, including the Buddha, reflect a growing proficiency in producing large works of art.

Inscriptions

Towards the end of the fifth century AD, kings in the delta region began to set up inscriptions to record their religious foundations. Only a handful survive, but their Sanskrit texts provide important information. The mutilated first few lines of the inscription from Go Thap, for example, cite a person whose name began with 'Ja', probably Jayavarman, who had been victorious in battle against a king whose name began with 'Vira'. *Varman* is a significant part of a royal name, for in Sanskrit it means shield or protector. This individual founded many sanctuaries dedicated to Vishnu, as was the one that he placed in the charge of his son Gunavarman. It had been 'wrested from the mud', possibly an allusion to the drainage of the Plain of Reeds where the inscription was set up. The consecration of this sanctuary was undertaken by Brahmans versed in the sacred texts. A second inscription from Nak Ta Dambang Dek was set up in honour of Buddha. It cites a King Jayavarman and his son Rudravarman (protected by Shiva), and describes how the former named the son of a Brahman as his inspector of property. A third text again mentions King Jayavarman and his victories won over rivals. The principal purpose of the inscription, however, was to record the foundation of a hermitage, a reservoir and a residence by his queen, Kulaprabhavati. *Kula* means family, *prabhavat* in Sanskrit may be translated as majesty.

Thus we learn that in the period AD 480–520, there were wars involving rival kings, the establishment of religious foundations in favour of exotic Indic gods, the presence of educated officiants and a royal succession from father to son. There are two inscriptions from the vicinity of Angkor Borei which imply that this was the capital of Rudravarman of Funan, the last recorded king in this region. One comes from Phnom Da and mentions his name on several occasions. The Prah Kuha Luon inscription dates to AD 674 and describes a local foundation by Rudravarman.

Agriculture

Although the Mekong Delta was well placed to exploit the southern silk route, its annual flood would have made rice cultivation difficult. Thus, no prehistoric settlements have been found on the flat delta terrain. While we know from Kang Tai that the people of Funan cultivated rice, we do not know how it was achieved. It is, however, possible that flooding was turned to the advantage of the rice farmers. In the first place, the flood waters regularly laid down silt, which enriched the fields and even made cultivation by ploughing or hoeing unnecessary. Provided that some surplus water could be retained behind artificial embankments or within natural basins, it would have been possible to undertake flood retreat cultivation. This technique, still to be seen in southern Cambodia, involves releasing the stored water regularly into the fields during the course of the early dry season. It is known to produce the high yields vital to sustain city life.

A major cultural change occurred in the delta of the Mekong River, beginning about AD 150. For centuries, mainland South-East Asian communities had been enlarging their trade contacts with increasingly distant countries, a trend sustained by their skill in maritime technology. The delta was not unique in this, for we find similar port societies developing in central Thailand and coastal Vietnam to form links in a chain that joined China with the Roman empire. Their origins involved warfare between competing states.

Increasing social complexity saw the establishment of large settlements, such as Oc Eo and Angkor Borei, linked to each other by a series of canals, which probably facilitated drainage and made possible the movement of trade goods. Large brick and stone monuments were certainly being built by the sixth century and possibly 200 years earlier. At the same time, stone statues were erected within settlements, with the Hindu god Vishnu being favoured.

Although many exotic items have been recovered, the settlements were themselves centres of specialist manufacture. All would have been sustained by rice surpluses. The organization and deployment of such resources would probably have involved a central administration, a clue to the nature of its leadership. The Chinese reported leaders with the title *fan*, but by the fifth century, the honorific title -*varman* was also used.

It is not yet possible to determine whether the delta maintained a single, unified state between AD 150 and 550, or rather whether there was a cluster of small and competitive polities vying for ascendancy. The existence of a network of interconnecting canals linking settlements as large as Oc Eo, Da Noi and Angkor Borei is reasonable but not conclusive evidence in favour of a single political entity. Whichever the case, a major stimulus to the emergence of social elites must have been participation in an international trade network, which gave leaders the opportunity to control trade and amass wealth and status. This trend did not occur in isolation, for many resources were drawn from the hinterland, where increasing production and competition would have provided local stimuli to the development of leadership. Noen U-Loke, occupied until about AD 400, is a site where we can trace the pattern of increasing social complexity in the interior lowlands that were affected by the developments on the delta.

The system, however, was fragile to the extent that it depended on a continuation of trading activity. Any downturn would have threatened its survival. At Angkor Borei, Stark has identified a peak in cultural activity during the occupation phase of Oc Eo, followed by marked changes manifested by fewer inscriptions and statues. This, she has suggested, might be the result of growing political power in centres to the north. These changes may also be linked with the documented alteration in the sea routes linking China with the West. They began during the fifth century, which saw the establishment of direct links with Java, at the expense of the Mekong Delta. For a state reliant upon the control of trade, this was a body blow. Sites like Oc Eo were abandoned by the sixth or seventh centuries AD, but the new situation, rather than seeing the end of the journey towards the civilization of Angkor, rather set the stage for major changes further up the valley of the Mekong and beside the Great Lake.

CHAPTER 4

THE EARLY KINGDOMS OF CHENLA:
AD 550–800

A thirteenth-century compilation by the Chinese author Ma Duanlin of available documents incorporates a description of an early seventh-century ruler, probably King Ishanavarman. It conjures an image of a sumptuous court, protected by armed guards. The king gave an audience every three days in a hall containing a wooden throne embellished with columns of inlaid wood and fine fabrics. He wore a crown of gold and precious stones, and golden ear pendants. Courtiers and officials touched the ground three times with their heads below the steps leading up to the throne. At the end of the audience, members of the court prostrated themselves.

This court was probably located at a place known today as Sambor Prei Kuk, in the Sen River valley east of the Great Lake of central Cambodia. The description reveals a complex social hierarchy steeped in wealth and ritual, the ingredients of civilization. The great ministers, said Ma Duanlin, number five, and there are many lesser officials. Today, one can still admire the concentration of temples and basins set within enclosing walls. There are three main groups, as well as a large *baray* and many temples outside the walled precincts. Inscriptions record that this centre was formerly known as Ishanapura, the city of Ishanavarman. Ma Duanlin's description brings this society to life: we learn that the people assiduously cleaned their teeth with poplar wood toothpicks, wore ear pendants and were of 'lively and robust temperament'. They always carried arms, and quarrels often involved fighting.

The Chinese records suggest that the decline of Funan on the Mekong Delta took place as leaders in the interior began to assert independent power, and they called the inland state Chenla. However, archaeological research and the study of inscriptions reveal several kingdoms, at least one of which rose to prominence even during the period of Funan. At a point 550 kilometres north of the delta, the Mekong River flows past a mountain peak notable for the natural *linga* or phallus-shaped rock at its summit. This auspicious mountain was recognized during the period of Angkor (from AD 800) by the construction of a temple complex known as Wat Phu, but it was also a major centre much earlier. An inscription at Wat Phu dated to the second half of the fifth century AD names a King Devanika, meaning celestial protection or divine inspiration. He came to rule there from afar as supreme king of kings, having obtained victory over innumerable enemies. His celebratory rituals involved, he said, the donation of thousands of cattle. The site of this inscription incorporates the rectangular outline of an early city.

A noble family

The next two centuries witnessed major developments in the river valleys of the interior and along the course of the Mekong River. Several Frenchmen, including Étienne Aymonier and Henri Parmentier, travelled extensively in this area and recorded many Chenla brick temples with their accompanying inscriptions. One such stela from the small sanctuary of Kdei Ang, set up in AD 667, bridges the transition from Funan to Chenla. It gives the names of successive members of an elite family and the kings they served. It begins with Brahmadatta, a retainer of King Rudravarman of Funan (about AD 514–50). The text then records his maternal nephews, Dharmadeva and Simhadeva, who served Kings Bhavavarman I and Mahendravarman. Simhavira, a maternal nephew of Dharmadeva, was an official under King Ishanavarman. Finally, Simhadatta served King Jayavarman I. King Ishanavarman took a wife from this lineage and had two sons, one being the future King Bhavavarman

II, the other, Shivadatta, being appointed the governor of Jyesthapura.

This text not only suggests that there was a smooth transition, in terms of administration, between the last recorded king of the delta state and his successors, but also reveals a dynastic succession. We know little of Bhavavarman I. He is referred to as the son of King Viravarman and the grandson of Sarvabhauma. An inscription from the site of Roban Romas mentions him as the overlord of Narasimhagupta, the King of Indrapura. It appears likely that his court was located at or near Ishanapura, and that he died in about AD 600. His brother, Mahendravarman, claimed victories in a series of short Sanskrit inscriptions set up in the Mun Valley to the north. The occupants of this area during the first decades of the seventh century were participants in the developing social complexity, their own emerging rulers almost certainly growing in wealth on the basis of rice, salt and iron production. The inscriptions of Mahendravarman need not imply more than exploratory or raiding expeditions, and there is no evidence that they involved permanent occupation and imposition of central authority. However, it is evident that he had territorial ambitions over a considerable area, and mustered sufficient force to campaign well beyond his base, which was almost certainly in the Sen Valley.

Significant structural changes in society took place during the reign of his son, Ishanavarman. The concentration of dedicatory inscriptions at his capital, let alone the actual name of this centre, make it clear that most of the buildings there were erected during his reign. The scale of Ishanapura indicates a substantial expenditure of energy and deployment of labour. There is also a consistent thread of evidence that Ishanavarman established some form of hegemony over strategic areas. In the far west, he appointed his son to rule over Jyesthapura. Closer to home, a text from Roban Romas describes how Narasimhagupta, the ruler of Indrapura, survived to become a vassal of Mahendravarman and Ishanavarman. He appointed a ruler of Tamandarapura, which was probably located in the delta region, and at Kuk Prah Kot, *pon*

Bhadrayuddha acknowledged Ishanavarman's supremacy. The ruler of Tamrapura recognized the overlordship of Ishanavarman, and recorded this in an inscription at Wat Chakret in AD 627. After defeating a rebellious prince, Ishanavarman also claimed authority over three other places, named as Cakrankapura, Amoghapura and Bhimapura. Here, we encounter at least three tiers of political authority, from Ishanavarman to Tamrapura and so to these three dependencies. Wat Po lies about 250 kilometres south of Ishanapura, and has provided an inscription by Ishanadatta which, having referred to the illustrious and heroic Ishanavarman, records the erection of an image for the benefit of his parents, with an endowment of many blocks of land from various high-status men bearing the honorific title *pon*. An inscription from Ishanapura itself describes the valour and military prowess of Ishanavarman, a king 'who extended the territory of his parents'.

Even if regional chiefs continued to exercise some independence in day-to-day affairs, Ishanavarman, who died shortly after AD 637, controlled considerable territory, including access to the sea via the Mekong and the Bang Pakong rivers. He was succeeded by his son Bhavavarman II, about whom little is known, save that he continued from the region of Ishanapura to maintain control over most, if not all, his father's fiefs. Even so, a number of inscriptions record foundations by local leaders without any reference to this king, a situation that might well indicate pockets of independence.

Jayavarman I

Jayavarman I (c. AD 635-80) was the great-grandson of Ishanavarman I. His inscriptions are concentrated in the lowlands bordering the Mekong River, extending north of the Great Lake and west into the rich agricultural area of Battambang. The various texts indicate his tightening of central power and control over a considerable area, his creation of new titles and administrators, and his ability to muster an army – the means of defence and destruction. Through the administrative structure, the king was able to issue orders bearing on land ownership and the payment of taxes. Although the actual location of his capital, Purandarapura, has yet to be identified, Vickery has suggested that an inscription from Tuol Kok Prah was probably close to the political centre of this capital. It describes Jayavarman as the conqueror of the circle of his enemies and recounts how Jnanacandra, an official (amatya) of high birth, erected an image of the god Amratakesvara. The assets of this foundation were joined by royal command with those of another god, the venerable and ancient Rudramahalaya. As the crow flies, Wat Po Val is just over 300 kilometres to the west of this inscription, although Cœdès noted that it might have been moved there from an unknown source. If one discounts the hyperbole typical of this genre, the inscription records warfare: King Jayavarman's commands were obeyed by 'innumerable vassal kings. In combat, he was a living incarnation of victory, the scourge of his enemies, lord of the land inherited from his ancestors, and conqueror of yet more lands.'

Wat Prei Val lies to the south of Tuol Kok Prah. An inscription there mentions the glorious King Jayavarman, and specifies that he ordered that Subhakirti, the great-nephew of the two founders, should have exclusive rights over the donations made by his great-uncles, including the animals, slaves and land, forests and fields. 'Those who disobey this royal order will be punished.' Again, the existence of a central authority is reflected in an inscription from Tuol Prah That, where Jayavarman is described as the destroyer of his enemies. The king appointed the author of the text as rajasabhapadi, president of the royal court, and honoured him with a white parasol and a golden vase. He erected a great linga called Kedaresvara. The king joined him and his nephews in endowing the foundation with fields, gardens, cattle, many buffaloes and slaves.

Jayavarman also strengthened the legal code. The cave of Prah Kuha Luon has furnished an inscription dated to AD 674, in which an edict (rajna) of King Jayavarman, from the palace at Purandarapura, confirms that the fields, cattle, buffaloes, servants and gardens are owned by ascetics and not by any private person. It carries imprecations against a large variety of possible crimes for which the king has provided punishment: 'Those who levy an annual tax, those who seize carts, boats, slaves, cattle, buffaloes, those who contest the king's orders, will be punished.'

The vital text from Wat Kdei Ang reveals a dynasty of royal retainers, which over at least four generations links the rule of Rudravarman of Funan to that of Jayavarman. A further inscription from Tan Kran describes how the king's court included a Brahman called Dharmasvami from Dharmapura. His lineage held the priestly position of *hotar*. His eldest son served the king as great master of the horse, and was given the governorship of Sresthapura with many honours, including a white parasol. He then became governor of Dhruvapura, a place of terrible forests and savages, where he established peaceful conditions. His younger brother was given a succession of high offices: officer of the royal guard, custodian of royal regalia, chief of the rowers and finally, by order of the king, he was placed in command of 1000 soldiers from Dhanvipura.

There is also a reference in an inscription from Wat Baray to the appointment of a *samantagajapadi*, chief of the royal elephants. The role of elephants in war is well documented in later centuries, so this person was probably a military leader. The king also appointed *mratan* (high official) and *pon* to a *sabha*, or council of state. Unfortunately, a further inscription, which mentions the chief of the royal grain stores (*dhanyakarapati*), is neither dated nor provenanced, but the style of the script indicates a date in this general period. This official was sufficiently wealthy to make a munificent gift for merit to a temple, including workers whose duties are specified. One was probably the leader; others included rice field labourers, spinners, weavers, singers, dancers, musicians, cooks, possibly smiths and grinders. It seems likely that the instigator was interested in the future supply of labour, for he lists the children of the female workers, even very young infants. Finally, a text from Tuol Nak Ta Bak Ka, which probably dates to this reign, prescribes the quantities of salt to be distributed by barge to various foundations, and prohibits any tax on the vessels going up or down river.

These sources suggest that Jayavarman I intensified the royal control over dependent fiefs that was begun by his great-grandfather, Ishanavarman I. He may also have shown increasing interest in the region north of the Tonle Sap, for here there is evidence for the rule of his successor, his daughter Queen Jayadevi. This royal lineage thereafter loses visibility in the historic records but did not necessarily terminate, since inscriptions dating to the greater part of the eighth century became very rare.

Other dynasties

Although it is possible to pinpoint places that acknowledged the overlordship of the Ishanapura kings and their successors, other kingdoms were independent. One centred on Stung Treng and followed the course of the Mekong possibly as far north as the confluence with the Mun River. An inscription dated AD 803 from Wat Tasar Moroy described a royal dynasty beginning with King Indraloka, who was succeeded by his daughter Nrpendradevi, granddaughter Jayendra...bha and her daughter Jyestharya. Doubtless their independence and wealth turned on controlling river passage and trade. A second kingdom, known as Canasapura, was located in the upper Mun area. An inscription from Ayutthaya mentions a King Bhagadatta and his successors, Sundaraparakrama, Sundaravarman, Narapatisimhavarman and Mangalavarman. All were members of the same family over several generations.

The social hierarchy

The brick shrines constructed during the seventh and eighth centuries were associated with local elites and royal rulers. A lintel from Wat En Khna shows a king in his throne chamber, surrounded by members of his court. In attempting to determine the social status and role of these people, the inscriptions are a vital source of information, since they provide names of individuals, their various titles and duties, and details of the economic transactions that took place within the context of the temple. Many royal names combined exalted Sanskrit words such as *jaya* (victory), or *mahendra* (the great Indra) with the title -*varman* linked with the title *raja* (king) or *maharaja* (great king) in Sanskrit and *vrah kamraten an* (royal and divine) in Khmer. The styles -*aditya*, the rising sun, and -*isvara* (lord) were employed in the names of kings. Sanskrit names and titles were always reserved for those of high status, although the Khmer title *vrah kamraten an* was also used for gods, suggesting that there was a strong ritual and ancestral element in the role of these kings. Courtiers and others of high status were accorded a variety of titles. The honorific term *mratan* was employed only for males. One married the daughter of King Ishanavarman, another the sister of Queen Jayadevi. There is no evidence for the title being inherited, yet *mratan* were given positions of considerable responsibility. Thus, a *mratan klon* was given official territorial duties, and a more highly ranked *mratan kurun* was the ruler of a territory. Their relationship to the king is seen in the secondment of a *mratan klon* to rule Jyesthapura under Ishanavarman: it was a royal appointment to a strategic but distant place. Other *mratan* are encountered as founders of or donors to temples, and all have Sanskrit names.

The title *pon*, probably the same title as *fan* mentioned by the Chinese, occurs in Khmer inscriptions from the earliest found until AD 719. The title appears to have been inherited, making it possible for an individual to be both a *pon* and *mratan*, and for the former to occupy a broad band in the social spectrum depending on their rank and wealth. Thus, Ishanavarman's son Shivadatta bore this title. Some *pon* acted on behalf of the king in the foundation of a temple, but others did so on their own initiative. The inscriptions reveal how *pon* assumed political and religious leadership in local affairs. They controlled the organization of rice production and the deployment of surpluses, took a keen interest in land title and boundaries, and oversaw the provision of labour in servicing the physical and ritual needs of their temples. *Pon* are often cited as controlling ponds and swamps, both critical in rural Cambodia, then as now, in the face of the long dry season. Vickery's detailed examination of the inscriptions has revealed that this title was inherited through the female line. A *pon* under this system was succeeded by his sister's son. The title became rare as inscriptions began to describe the new titles and bureaucratic positions established in the reign of Jayavarman I.

Both within the royal centres and deep in the rural hinterlands, a social system acknowledging hereditary rank had developed by the early seventh century. The kings themselves surely derived their political and ritual powers from within this framework. The rulers, members of their court and local leaders could not exist in a vacuum. What do the inscriptions tell us of other members of society? Women played central roles in rituals. Some bore the title *tan* (a minor official), others were named in conjunction with a title indicating high status. There was also a wide range of crafts carried out by male and female specialists. They include workers of iron, sewers of leaves, herdsmen, cooks, perfume grinders, spinners and weavers. One unique term might describe a moulder of statues. The names given to artisans also provide insight into their skills, such as basket maker, and the mention of particular products reveals specialist output: gold, bronze, a copper gong, a diadem, an umbrella, many types of pottery vessel and varieties of woven cloth. Agricultural labourers were mentioned most frequently for, in the final analysis, it was rice that fuelled the social engine. While the elite had Sanskrit names, the majority were known by Khmer names.

Society was thus increasingly divided into elite and junior lineages, the latter already, or soon to become, commoners. Leaders were responsible for the construction of temples which housed ancestral spirits or gods. The ancestral and local deities, often female, were called *kpon*. Highly ranked descent from their ancestors and close identity with the gods involved *pon* in ritual and cult duties to which all members of the community adhered. The textual records indicate that *pon* were in a position to donate communal land to the temple. They also assigned their juniors to provide surplus agricultural and craft products. But since it was they who founded and maintained the temple, this meant that they also deployed surplus production. For the elite, this system involved the accumulation of wealth in the form of rice, cloth and land. For the majority of society, who lacked the status to acquire Sanskrit names, it involved producing a surplus for the benefit of the temple and ancestral gods, and an ideological dividend in the idea of making merit. It is important to note that the elevation of an elite segment of society into a permanent position of economic and ideological management is an essential building block in the foundation of states.

The temple

Most temples were raised on a platform and enclosed a square, rectangular or occasionally octagonal chamber. The brick super-structure rose narrow and tall into a corbelled vault, while the interior housed a *linga* and statues of deities. The temple exterior was usually decorated, most prominently in the form of a large sandstone lintel over the entrance with supporting carved stone columns. Early lintels were often embellished with a mythical monster known as a *makara*, together with medallions usually illustrating the god Indra. In later examples, the *makara* was replaced by floral decoration.

Brick was the preferred building material, but stone was used for door and window frames. The holes for hanging wooden doors often survive, but false doors were usually inserted on other walls, along with pilasters and floral or geometric decoration. Representations of miniature buildings were often incorporated in the panels between pilasters, and these provide some insight into elite domes-tic structures or the nature of palaces. An example from Ishanapura, easily the largest site of this period, shows elevated and richly decorated pavilions with windows separated by columns. Figures can be seen within, presumably members of the aristocracy. Some temples stand alone, but others are grouped. At Ishanapura, decorated brick walls surround groups of temples and water basins.

Stone inscriptions set into these monuments provide a vital social overlay to the skeletal archaeological remains. These usually incorporate, in Sanskrit, the name or names of the founders, the presiding god, and the date. Further information follows in Khmer. The names of the king or benefactor and the god are repeated. Although Hindu gods are often named, with a preference for Shiva, local gods, probably of considerable antiquity, are also mentioned. We find reference to the god of the cloud, a tree, the old and the young god, and the god at the double pond or in the west. Many deities, or *kpon*, were localised in distribution and might have been ancestral, family gods. A typical inscription will then list the amount of land ascribed to the temple; its boundaries, value and productive capacity; the names of people assigned to maintain the temple and their duties; and finally, a warning against transgressing the rules governing the foundation. Although the archaeological record on domestic and secular aspects of these communities is silent, we can nevertheless turn to the inscriptions for some insight into the nature of society and its economic foundations.

Because they were constructed in permanent materials, temple sanctuaries have survived. (However excavations are needed to assess the extent of other buildings, for one might reasonably expect there to have been wooden houses for priests and other temple functionaries, storage facilities and palaces.) The inscriptions certainly reveal that temples were far more than places of worship, as we can quickly perceive if we consider them from the point of view of first the *pon* and their relatives and then the assigned workers. For the former, the temple was the focus for rites relating to local and ancestral gods. Leading the senior lineage, and therefore being closest to the ancestors, the *pon* had a powerful role to play in mediating with the spirits. This central function is possibly hard for pragmatic Western readers to appreciate, yet this reverence continues to this day. Before excavating a prehistoric site in modern Thailand or Cambodia, archaeologists must make offerings to the spirits. Spirit houses are everywhere, and attract daily offerings of food and flowers. When there is a plague of crabs or insects in the rice fields, the farmer appeals to the spirits.

If land was in corporate rather than personal ownership, then it was logically temple property. It would be to the advantage of the *pon* if the land were made as productive as possible, because he and his entourage would be sustained by the surplus production, while also ensuring that some was available for meritorious donations and trade. One foundation might have a surplus of rice, another of cloth, a third of fruit or ironware. So *pon*, through the medium of the temple, could organize trade of these surpluses not only for basic food and cloth, but also for bankable assets, such as gold and silver.

Administrators of a wealthy foundation could thus build up sufficient capital to buy further land, even another temple, or they could merge their assets through marriage alliances. For the ambitious leader, this could represent a route to the accumulation of considerable wealth and power, even to the status of royalty. This is one reason why established kings took such a keen interest in the amalgamation of temples and in the rights to land ownership. On the one hand, land could be used to reward loyalty, but on the other, it could be accrued to the point where the owner became a potential rival. All this, however, turned on controlling sufficient labour for efficient production, whether in the clearance of forests and the creation of rice fields, the forging of iron tools, the provision of domestic stock or the construction of water tanks to satisfy domestic needs during the dry season.

Labour was therefore an essential requirement, and it is not surprising to find detailed lists of workers, their number, names and duties. Some of these labourers might have been war captives, but the majority were probably junior kin of the *pon*. Assessing their motivation to produce surpluses for the *pon* to dispose of entails a degree of speculation. There can be little doubt, however, that one compelling issue was the notion of merit making. This required what Colin Renfrew has summarised as 'investment in charismatic authority'. By working more than was necessary for basic subsistence and providing thereby a surplus for the ancestral spirits represented in their temple, the *knum* were making merit for themselves. They received the benediction of the ancestors, their intervention to ensure the arrival of the rains and, in the event of a poor harvest, the assurance that the *pon* would provide for their needs, for example through the exchange of accumulated valuables for food from more fortunate institutions.

It is, therefore, hardly surprising in this agrarian society that there are numerous references to the boundaries of rice fields under the jurisdiction of *pon*. Many bordered a *travan* (that is, an artificial pond), or roads, or forests. Again, there are lists of temple assets including animals, surplus agricultural production, officiants, musicians and dancers, and craft specialists. The founders of the temple, or other named beneficiaries, held rights to gifts made to the temple and, in the case of land, its usufruct. Although *pon* accumulated and exchanged their assets, there was no system of coinage. Goods were valued by reference to the weight of silver, or a quantity of rice or the length and quality of cloth. An inscription from Lonvek records the assignment of 17 dancers or singers, 23 or 24 record keepers, 19 leaf sewers, 37 artisans including a potter, 11 weavers, 15 spinners and 59 rice field workers of whom 46 were female.

This gender imbalance among rice field workers poses the issue of how agriculture was undertaken. There is no reference to irrigation in the inscriptions, making it likely that flood retreat agriculture or the inundation system, relying on rainfall to fill bunded rice fields, were practised. Was the soil prepared by human labour, or with the aid of the plough and traction animals? The latter is much more productive, but there are no references to ploughs in the inscriptions. There are, however, many allusions to water buffalo being assigned to temples; there is reference to a yoke in one inscription; and ploughing with yoked cattle is depicted on the bas-reliefs of Borobudur in Java dating to *c.* AD 780. The predominance of women over men in the tally of rice field workers seen above might provide a further clue. If men were undertaking the ploughing and harrowing, and women were responsible for transplanting, as is the case today, then presumably most of the people in this text listed as artisans could have been men. A second system might have been practised in low-lying terrain where flooding was so deep and prolonged as to rule out wet season cultivation. The flood retreat system, already described for the delta state of Funan, followed during historic times in areas that saw major settlement during the period of Chenla kingdoms. It involves the retention of flood water in natural swamps or behind artificial bunds, which is released into rice fields during the dry season. The annual deposition of silt not only fertilized the rice fields, but also made ploughing unnecessary.

The texts also reveal that economic transactions were considerably more complicated than a simple donation of land and its products to a communal temple for the elite to manage. There are records of assets being exchanged between individuals through the aegis of the temple management. On occasion, we find that land was mortgaged, as it were, to a temple in return for silver or cloth, and the product of the land was assigned as a form of interest payment. A donor might gift products to the temple, but receive other goods in return, or deposit goods against which to make a later claim. The temple, then, performed a key role in the appropriation of a community asset into a medium for the creation and exchange of wealth items among the elite. The stone inscriptions are probably a thin veneer reflecting major transactions, under which temple records accumulated on less durable media, such as palm leaves.

The concentration of power

An intensification of the concentration of economic and ideological power in the hands of local elites brings with it three implications. The first, and in many ways the most critical, was the social norm for the inheritance of status and property. Vickery's detailed analysis of inheritance rules during the period when *pon* were flexing their social muscles has revealed a major difficulty facing the accumulation of wealth and assets within an essentially matrilineal system. The title and status of the *pon* was transmitted not to a male heir, but to his sister's son. Therefore an aspiring leader could not bequeath his wealth to his direct descendants. This rule of succession ran counter to the formation of large, centrally directed states. The mould was broken in the expansive dynasty of Ishanapura, in which rulers assumed the style of gods and were succeeded in the male line, although inheritance through a man's maternal nephew continued for centuries even in elite families. A second solution, seen in the polity of Sambhupura, was to permit succession directly through the female line. In both cases, the lateral transmission of assets and leadership through the ruler's sister and so to the next generation was bypassed.

The second issue is the increase in central, royal power, and the alienation of land and its produce from communal ownership. Royal leaders were being accorded the divine title, *vrah kamraten an*. One inscription refers to Bhavavarman I, Mahendravarman and Ishanavarman I by this title, but at the time it was written, they were already deceased. Jayavarman I in AD 664 was the first king to be recorded with this divine title during his own lifetime. It is not, therefore, surprising to find that he also superseded the regional *pon* in determining the disposition of temple assets. In the same inscription containing this title, he ordered that the assets of the Wat Prei Val be for the exclusive benefit of the grand-nephew of the founder. Seventeen years later, he decreed that the wealth of a second temple could not be owned by the descendants of the founder. The disposition of assets, in other words, could be controlled by the king.

With this centralization of authority, the number of inscriptions was drastically reduced at a time when the arts and architecture flourished. There is, therefore, a gap in our knowledge of political development between AD 720 and 770, only partially filled by retrospective texts. An inscription from Wat Khnat, Siem Reap, mentions a king named Nrpaditya, who was alive not long after the rule of Jayavarman I. A second text from Ampil Rolum described three eighth-century kings, also with names ending in

-aditya (the rising sun), ruling at Bhavapura. The wealth of detail contained in the seventh-century texts, however, is missing.

The period between AD 550 and 800 witnessed the formation of a series of states in the low-lying interior of Cambodia, an area well suited to an agrarian economy. Flood retreat agriculture in low-lying fields annually replenished with silt could well have provided the necessary rice surpluses to sustain the social elite. This period saw the creation of wealth, which was accumulated by this elite to their own advantage, through the aegis of the communal temple. Surpluses of cloth, rice and measures of silver and gold were media for exchange, but the coinage seen in the Funan state was no longer in circulation. Warfare is a recurrent theme in the inscriptions, and it is possible to trace the fortunes of several dynasties. The most successful appears to have been based, for part of its life, at Ishanapura in the valley of the Sen River. Later Chinese texts describe the royal palace, and many temples and a large reservoir still survive there. Other states are less well documented, although three successive queens are known from Sambhupura.

For a century from AD 611, the Khmer language inscriptions refer to *pon*, a hereditary title for a highly ranked member of society. Some endowed their ancestral foundations with land, labour, stock and the officiants necessary for rituals. They had Sanskrit names, whereas the labourers bore names in Khmer. Reference to *pon* ceased early in the eighth century, at a time when the title *mratan*, which was evidently conferred by a king, became increasingly common. Jayavarman I exercised his authority over a substantial territory. The inscriptions reveal that he bestowed a growing number of administrative titles and the provision of symbols of status, such as white parasols, to his appointees. He also had control over military force, which he used to maintain and expand his kingdom.

The use of Sanskrit for elite personal names, some titles, major centres and deities has given the false impression that the states of Chenla were deeply penetrated by Indian religions and political philosophy. On the contrary, an Indic veneer covered local cults and deities, and the change of names was more a self-interested use of the exotic to enhance personal prestige.

The number of inscriptions declined sharply during the eighth century, and the dynasty represented by Jayavarman I loses visibility with the reign of his daughter Jayadevi. The reasons for this virtual lacuna are unclear, but later records which refer retrospectively to this period leave us in no doubt that there continued to be kings, that temples were still being endowed and that conflict was the rule rather than the exception.

CHAPTER 5

THE DYNASTY OF JAYAVARMAN II:
AD 800–1000

In about AD 800, a king named Jayavarman II laid the foundations of a state and a dynasty that endured for two centuries. From this period on, the state was called Kambujadesa, or Cambodia. He ruled from the land between the northern shore of the Great Lake and the Kulen uplands. The lake supplied limitless fish while regular flooding encouraged the cultivation of rice. In many respects, the founding king and members of this new dynasty achieved the objectives of his predecessor, Jayavarman I. They presented the image of a unified kingdom, which encompassed the rich lowlands flanking the Mekong River to the delta, the Great Lake and the fine agricultural land of Battambang to the west. Successive court centres were located beyond the flood zone of the Great Lake. They incorporated increasingly large and impressive temples dedicated to the sovereign and his ancestors, and *barays* fed by the rivers issuing from the sacred Kulen upland. There were also palaces and secular buildings, although being made of wood, they have not survived.

Jayavarman II set a precedent to be followed by his successors, by having himself consecrated king of kings in a highly charged ritual ceremony. He surrounded himself with court officials whose ceremonial duties, such as bearing the royal fan or fly whisk, were to be jealously guarded by their descendants. The court was projected as the centre of the kingdom and a representation of heaven, but was sustained by the agricultural surpluses. The inscriptions are filled not only with references to the elite aristocrats and their meritorious acts, but also contain details of land ownership, field boundaries and the duties of retainers. We find many references to slaves, but it would be wrong to regard this as a slave-based society. The rural populace donated part of their time and labour to maintain the local temple. Thus part of their production, be it rice, butter, honey, cloth or livestock, was directed to the capital. Our knowledge of this, the first dynasty of Angkor, comes from the inscriptions, reservoirs and surviving stone or brick temples. On the one hand, we encounter a dynasty of kings who built on an increasingly massive scale and extended their power through elite aristocrats to the sustaining populace. On the other hand, we find endemic instability rooted in disputes within a dynasty that had no clear rules to govern the succession, and the constant problem of maintaining control over the provinces.

Jayavarman II and the establishment of royal power

The origins and achievements of Jayavarman II remain shrouded in a mist that only intensive archaeological research and the for-tuitous discovery of further inscriptions can disperse. Two inscriptions find him, during the last two decades of the eighth century, on the east bank of the Mekong some distance from the old royal centre of Ishanapura. Of aristocratic origin, he probably began his career at or near Vyadhapura, Banteay Prei Nokor.

In 1936, Victor Goloubew, who worked for the École Française d'Extrême-Orient, took a series of aerial photographs of this site, in which the temples, bank and moat stand out clearly. He also noted five reservoirs on the same axis, all outside the moat, and a road linking the site with the Mekong River to the west. Today, the huge enclosure remains demarcated by its encircling walls and moat, while brick shrines dominate its centre. Excavations are required to pursue the possibility that it dates to the period when Jayavarman II and his followers began their odyssey to the north-west which led to the foundation of Angkor. The next mention of him is found in an inscription dedicating a foundation

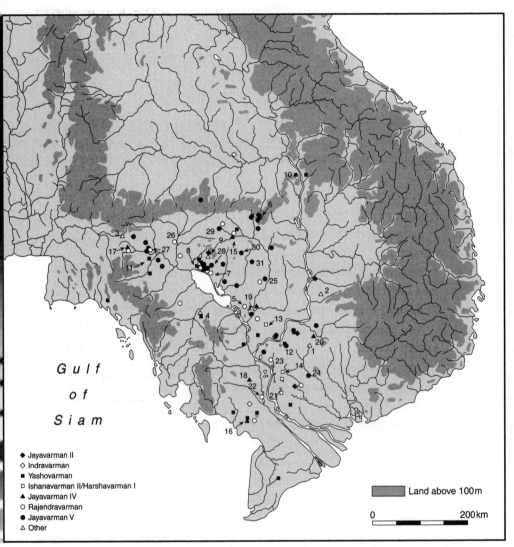

The distribution of inscriptions for the dynasty of Jayavarman II.

1 Banteay Prei Nokor, 2 Lobok Srot, 3 Sdok Kak Thom, 4 Palhal, 5 Thvar Kdei, 6 Prasat Kantop, Prasat Thnal Chuk, 7 Hariharalaya, 8 Ak Yum, Prei Kmeng, Prasat Kok Po, Prasat Khnat and Phnom Rung, 9 Rong Chen, 10 Wat Phu, 11 Prasat Kuk Pradak, 12 Phum Mien, 13 Tuol Pei, 14 Prah Vihear Kuk, 15 Chok Gargyar (Lingapura), 16 Phnom Bayang, 17 Nong Pang Puey, 18 Prasat Nan Khmau, 19 Ampil Rolum, 20 Con An, 21 Prasat Anlon Car, 22 Ba Phnom, 23 Kdei Skie, 24 Basak, 25 Ishanapura, 26 Tuk Cum, 27 Phnom Kanva, 28 Banteay Srei, 29 Prasat Komphus, 30 Phnom Mrec, 31 Tuol Prasat

at Lobok Srot, and describes Jayavarman as king of the earth surrounded by the ocean. This site, located in the area of Sambhupura, might well reflect a marriage alliance with the local queen.

For further information on Jayavarman II, we must turn to an inscription found at Sdok Kak Thom in eastern Thailand and dated 260 years later than the events described. It was put in place by Sadasiva, a member of an aristocratic priestly family who traced his ancestors back to the time of Jayavarman II. It describes how Jayavarman II returned from Java to rule in the holy city of Indrapura. The term Java has led to a wild-goose chase involving wars between the Khmer and Javanese, but the truth is probably less dramatic. Vickery has noted that the Khmer described their close neighbours, the Chams, as the *chvea*. Banteay Prei Nokor lies on the eastern marches of Cambodia, and a skirmish with the Chams is a more likely interpretation of this statement than a long sojourn in distant Java.

Shivakaivalya, the ancestor of the family described in the text, was a royal chaplain who had been in charge of a *linga* at Bhadrayogi in the district of Indrapura. The king ordered Shivakaivalya to move himself, his family and presumably their retainers to Purvadisa, where they were granted land and established a settlement called Kuti. Its location is unknown, but it was a considerable distance from Vyadhapura.

This move was not without incident. According to an inscription from Palhal in Battambang province, dating to AD 1069, Jayavarman's early years involved much conflict. He ordered the *mratan* Prithivinarendra to pacify all districts. Accompanied by two other leaders, he extinguished resistance in Malyang, modern Battambang. Jayavarman rewarded his generals with fine estates and the two leaders who accompanied Prithivinarendra settled there with their families. An inscription from Thvar Kdei in Kompong Thom province, dated 150 years after these events, records how the king endowed land to *vap* Jataveda, the chief of pages in the *sruk* of Sahakara. *Vap* is an honorific title which does not appear in any earlier record, its literal meaning probably being 'father'. A second retrospective text from Prasat Kantop records that one of Jayavarman's wives was granted land in this area, to found a village and settle her family and followers.

In the meantime, Jayavarman established himself at Hariharalaya on the northern margin of the Great Lake, an area noted for the potential of flood retreat agriculture. The brick sanctuaries at Trapeang Phong could well date from his stay there. We follow his peregrinations with a further move, this time to Amarendrapura. Again, the precise location is not known, but it may well have incorporated some of the impressive temples, built in the style of the period, that are concentrated at the western end of the Western Baray of Angkor. Here, excavations have uncovered a large temple complex at Ak Yum which was partially covered by the dyke of the Baray. This temple lay within a large rectangular enclosure known as Banteay Choeu. Goloubew (1936) noted further enclosures surrounding the temples of Prei Kmeng and Phnom Rung, respectively to the west and north of the Western Baray.

The transition from a single-chambered brick sanctuary to multiple towers on top of a raised series of platforms probably took place during the reign of Jayavarman II. Ak Yum is such a temple. Excavations by George Trouvé in 1935 exposed much of the central structure. The lowest platform was built up of earth with its major paths sealed in bricks. It was 100 metres square and 2.6 metres high. Access to the second stage was by stairs, which ascend 2.4 metres onto a platform constructed of bricks, 42 metres long on each side. The walls were decorated with images of miniature palaces similar to those of the preceding single-chambered structures. Indeed, this second stage incorporates a series of such brick towers embellished with sandstone false doors and lintels. An inscription from a stone sculpture near the southeast angle tower records a donation to the god Gamhiresvara in AD 1001. This god of the depths was popular at Ishanapura, and the text reveals the sanctity of this temple over a period of at least two centuries.

The main sanctuary on the third tier had one entrance facing east, but the other three walls were later provided with separate portals. The original lintel and columns date to the end of the eighth century AD. Two reused inscriptions from the central tower date to 704 and 717. The latter records a foundation by *mratan* Kirtigana to the god Gamhiresvara, and notes donations to the temple which include rice, draught cattle, cloth and workers. There can be no doubt that this area, so close to the future centre of Angkor, was occupied and farmed by the early eighth century.

The central chamber yielded six bronze statues, two of a Hindu deity and four of the Buddha, varying between 9 and 35 centimetres in height, and part of a large stone *linga*. The excavators then encountered an extraordinary vault leading to a subterranean chamber, the base of which was 12.5 metres below the floor of the central tower. It comprised a brick shrine dedicated, no doubt, to Gamhiresvara, god of the profound depths, and contained two elephants in gold leaf and a statue of a man standing 1.25 metres high.

The dating of the temple pyramid at Ak Yum is revealed first by the inscriptions, which indicate construction later than the early eighth century, and second by the architectural style. The consensus on the latter suggests a date in the second half of that century. This opens the possibility that it represents an enlargement in the size of temples dating to and perhaps inspired by Jayavarman II.

Ak Yum was one of several sanctuaries that were concentrated round the western end of the Western Baray. Four have been investigated beyond the northern dyke at Prasat Kok Po, where Monument C was built in the same style as Ak Yum. Monuments B, A and D at this site are stylistically slightly later. Prasat Khnat, a third site in this vicinity, may well date to an establishment of Jayavarman II.

In 1936, the French archaeologist Philippe Stern explored the forested Kulen upland, described in the inscriptions as Mahendraparvata, Mountain of the Great Indra. In five heady weeks, he explored hitherto unknown temples, fallen lintels and statues of Vishnu. He described the sanctuary of Rong Chen as the first true temple mountain, the central sanctuary being found on top of three terraces. It may have been the holy nature of this mountain that attracted Jayavarman, for he had himself consecrated the supreme king there, in the presence of an image of Shiva. The latter was named *kamraten jagat te raja*, or *devaraja*, the god who is king. This image accompanied successive rulers when on their journeys. The text notes that the ceremony ensured that Cambodia would be free from dependency upon Java (presumably the neighbouring Chams) and that there would be only one 'Lord of the lower earth' who would be the *chakravartin*, or universal overlord.

This upland area, visible on a clear day from Angkor, was the fecund source of the rivers that flow south to the Tonle Sap, but it must have been difficult to maintain a court and a following there, remote from good rice-growing terrain. Finally, Jayavarman closed the circle by descending to Hariharalaya, where he died about AD 835.

Jayavarman III

We know virtually nothing of Jayavarman's son and successor, Jayavarman III. An inscription from Prasat Sak, which comprises two brick sanctuaries just north of Siem Reap, ascribes the foundation of the temple to the year in which Jayavarman III ascended the throne. When he failed to capture a wild elephant while hunting, a divinity promised that he would secure the animal if he built a sanctuary. At least some other temples are known to date to the reign of Jayavarman III, indicating continuing interest in the region of Angkor. Due north of Ak Yum but on the opposite side of the Western Baray lies the temple of Prasat Kok Po. An inscription records the erection of a statue of Vishnu here by Prithivindrapandita, a *guru* of the king, in 857. Jayavarman III may also have initiated the construction of the Bakong at Hariharalaya. He died in 877 and was succeeded by Indravarman I.

Indravarman I

In his official genealogy, Indravarman did not mention any relationship with Jayavarman II or III, but at his temple of Preah Ko,
he dedicated shrines to Jayavarman II and his principal consort,
as well as his father and maternal grandfather and their wives.
Given the flexible rules governing the succession, it is hardly surprising that Indravarman's accession was contested. One of his
inscriptions says that 'the right hand of this prince, long and powerful, was terrible in combat when his sword fell on his enemies,
scattering them to all points of the compass. Invincible, he was
appeased only by his enemies who turned their backs in surren-
der, or who placed themselves under his protection.' This claim
was engraved on the foundation stela of the temple of Preah Ko in
AD 879. It was followed by a promise made on his accession: 'Five
days hence, I will begin digging.'

Indravarman lived up to his promise by having a huge *baray*
constructed, and recorded in another inscription: 'He made the
Indratataka, mirror of his glory, like the ocean.' Now dry, but
clearly visible from the air, this *baray* was of unprecedented size,
being 3800 metres long and 800 metres wide. It was created by
constructing dykes to retain the water flowing south from the
Kulen Hills. To augment its flow, he had part of the Roluos River
canalized and directed towards the *baray*. The northern dyke and
the Lolei temple in the middle of the reservoir (known as a
mebon) were completed by his son.

The purpose of these reservoirs remains controversial. Many
Western scholars assume that their size implies that they were
used for the irrigation of rice fields. But no inscription specifically
mentions this purpose, and it is possible that, quite apart from
supplying a constant source of water to the palace and temples,
they symbolized the oceans that surrounded Mount Meru, the
home of the gods. In this interpretation, the increasingly large and
impressive temple pyramids, dedicated to the royal ancestors,
represent Mount Meru itself.

Indravarman constructed two major temples at Hariharalaya to the south of his new reservoir. Their associated basins and moats were probably fed from the waters of·the Indratataka. They are known as the Preah Ko and the Bakong. Preah Ko is a recent name meaning sacred ox, after the statues of the bull Nandi, Shiva's sacred mount, which guard the entrance. The complex is surrounded by a 50-metre-wide moat, which encloses an area of 600 × 550 metres. To the east lies the Srah Andaung Preng, a basin 100 metres square. The open area between the moat and the wall of the second enclosure has not been investigated by archaeologists, but a rectangular platform on a north–south axis in the western precinct might well be the foundations for the royal palace. Indravarman's own inscription mentions in glowing terms his 'lion throne, a vehicle, the palace Indravimanaka and a golden pavilion'.

Access to the second court is effected through a laterite and sandstone *gopura*, that is, an entrance pavilion incorporating a gateway. The area within is dominated by a platform bearing six shrines. Still impressive in their size and harmony, they must have been doubly so when newly completed, for the brick walls were covered in layers of painted stucco. Their inscriptions reveal a political as well as a religious purpose. The three towers of the front row were dedicated to Rudravarman and Prithivindravarman, respectively Indravarman's maternal grandfather and father, with the central tower being dedicated to Jayavarman II.

Who was Indravarman, and what was his relationship to his predecessors? He said, in his foundation stela, that his mother was the daughter of Rudravarman, and granddaughter of Nrpatindravarman. His father was named Prithivindravarman, of noble lineage. For further details, we can turn to an inscription set up by a noble family at Wat Samrong. During the reign of Jayavarman II, a brother and two sisters from that family were respectively an army leader, the queen of Bhavapura and the wife of another general. Jayavarman required them to accompany him on his move to the Angkor region, marrying the first sister. One of their children, a daughter, then married a high-status man, and they themselves had a daughter, Narendra. She has therefore a granddaughter of Jayavarman II, and she became the wife of Indravarman. The byzantine relationships that unfold with this inscription continue. Indravarman's mother's brother married Jayavarman's daughter. So, Indravarman married his first cousin. Again, Indravarman's paternal grandmother was the younger sister of Jayavarman II's wife, making him the great-nephew by marriage of Jayavarman II and step first cousin once removed of Jayavarman III.

Each royal ancestor's name at Preah Ko was joined with that of Shiva, thus projecting the image of deified forebears. The three sanctuaries in the second row acknowledged Narendradevi, Prithivindradevi and Dharanindradevi, the principal consorts of each lord. Each shrine would have contained an image of the ancestor, and the goods donated by the king give some inkling of the splendour of this monument. This 'lion among kings of kings' donated palanquins, parasols, beautifully made vessels of gold and silver in many forms, gold and silver boxes, silver fans and jars, swords with gold hilts, libation vessels, mirrors with gold supports, fly whisks, precious perfumes, clothing and spears ornamented with silver. He also donated dancers, singers, musicians, many of them males, well clothed and talented; thousands of men and women field workers from numerous villages, and well-sited fields as well as thousands of cattle, buffaloes, goats, elephants and horses.

Whilst this temple might have been an ancestral chapel royal, the adjacent Bakong is far larger and of different construction and design. It may have begun as a laterite structure in the reign of Jayavarman III, but was completed under Indravarman I. The first innovation is the sheer scale of the conception: the central pyramid rises in five stages within a double-moated enclosure 800 metres square. The innermost moat is flanked by steep steps leading down to the water. Four *gopuras* give access to the central court, the principal eastern gate being linked to the pyramid by a causeway. An impression of size and scale is provided not only by the cyclopean masonry and statues of elephant guardians on the first three levels, but also by the five successive terraces rising 14 metres above ground level. Unfortunately, the summit shrine has not survived. In Indravarman's words: 'In 881, the king, like a god, dispenser of riches, has erected a *linga* named Indresvara, here.' This name combines that of the king with the god Shiva (esvara), indicating a submergence of the king within the deity into a single object of devotion.

The eight small sanctuaries placed uniformly round the base of the pyramid probably acknowledged male and female ancestors of Indravarman, for the eastern set incorporates male figures on the exterior niches but female on the western ones. The foundation stela relates that 'Here, in the court of Indravarman, causing joy to those who behold it and unreserved wonder of the celestial builder, he erected eight *lingas* named by royal practice after the eight elements of Shiva: earth, wind, fire, the moon, sun, water, ether and the sacrificer.' Still awesome today, to contemporaries versed in the Hindu canon the temple must have been a majestic symbol of royal power, for it would have been possible then to appreciate the relief carvings, of which only traces survive. The wall of the topmost tier reveals a battle scene involving a group of *asuras* or monsters. Indravarman's architects also employed, for the first time, the *naga*, a mythical serpent and guardian of earthly wealth, which also represented the rainbow, the bridge between the human world and the domain of the gods. The access bridge guarded by *nagas* marked the threshold from the profane to the sacred. Most significantly, the world within was dominated by the divine images of the king and his ancestors.

Yashovarman I

Yashovarman I succeeded his father in AD 889. His accession may not have been peaceful, for one of his inscriptions records a naval battle, which probably took place on the Tonle Sap. He is also described on many occasions as a powerful and victorious warrior. His father had opened a new dimension in the scale of the urban landscape with his additions to Hariharalaya, but these pale before the achievement of Yashovarman. He first completed the Indratataka by the construction of the northern dyke and the temple set on the island at Lolei. The four shrines there were dedicated to his father, his maternal grandfather, his mother and his maternal grandmother. The names of each combine that of the royal ancestor with a god. An addendum to a stela of Indravarman at Preah Ko details his assignment of goods and people to the temple. It includes gold, silver, servants from *sruk* Samrong, including five guardians of beasts, from *sruk* Abhinavagrama in *praman* Jen Taran and *sruk* Tampal in *praman* Malyan. The term *praman* is interesting, because it refers to a territory under the king's jurisdiction and rule. Since some of those territories mentioned are some distance from Hariharalaya, it would appear that Yashovarman wielded the necessary authority to appropriate and deploy goods and labour.

The distribution of his inscriptions reveals a kingdom that included the old heartland of Jayavarman I to the south and the strategic site of Wat Phu to the north-east. These would have ensured a measure of control over the vital Mekong waterway. It is also notable that settlements to the west of the Tonle Sap were consolidating, and that new foundations were springing up in the north-east.

Access to labour and agricultural surpluses was vital for Yashovarman's ambitious construction programme. About 18 kilometres to the north-west of the capital that he inherited lies a low hill known as the Bakheng. He chose this eminence for his central state temple, and surrounded the cult centre with a rectangular moat 4 kilometres square and 200 metres wide. Despite the many subsequent building programmes, the south-west corner of this moat is still visible on the ground and from the air. The Bakheng temple in the centre of the new city was itself ringed by a second moat measuring 650 × 436 metres, traversed by four *gopuras*. Access to the summit temple is by steep stairs, but the top of the hill has been partially levelled, so that the six terraces of the sanctuary rise from the plateau like a crown. There are numerous brick chapels at the base of the pyramid and on the terraces. The topmost tier incorporates a quincunx of temples, the largest in the centre and the others at each corner.

This new city of Yashodharapura was linked to Hariharalaya by a causeway, which reached the outer moat north of the main eastern entrance and then proceeded directly to the Bakheng. This implies that the second entrance probably ran parallel and to the north, giving access to the royal palace. Victor Goloubew noted both a physical and a stylistic link between the Bakong and the Bakheng, and is responsible for identifying the latter as the centre of Yashodharapura. Having studied the central temple and its surrounding moats from the air, he explored the faint traces of carriageways issuing from the former along the cardinal point of the compass. To the east, his excavations revealed laterite blocks lining the old road, flanked by water basins. Using his elephants to push through the thick vegetation at this point, he emerged into open rice fields to find again traces of this road. Goloubew then identified the roads that ran west, south and north from the base of the Bakheng, as well as the inner moat, which defines the hill. Further excavations uncovered roof tiles, suggesting that elite residences were located inside the outer moat. We do not know how much of the interior was settled, nor the size of the population. From every vantage point, however, the dominant towers of the Bakheng would have been a visible reminder of the cosmic power and majesty of the king.

The urban complex extended well beyond the outer moat. Yashovarman ordered the creation of the massive Yashodharatataka, or Eastern Baray, the dykes of which measure 7.5 × 1.8 kilometres. Inscriptions erected at each corner record this remarkable achievement which, when full, would have contained over 50 million cubic metres of water. The *baray* was fed by a canal linking it with the Siem Reap River, and it emptied into a canal that filled the moats of the city to the west. He also had at least four monasteries constructed south of his new reservoir, and temples on surrounding hills at Phnom Dei, Phnom Krom and Phnom Bok. He ordered the foundation of 100 *ashramas*, or retreats for ascetics, each with its rules of conduct set in stone.

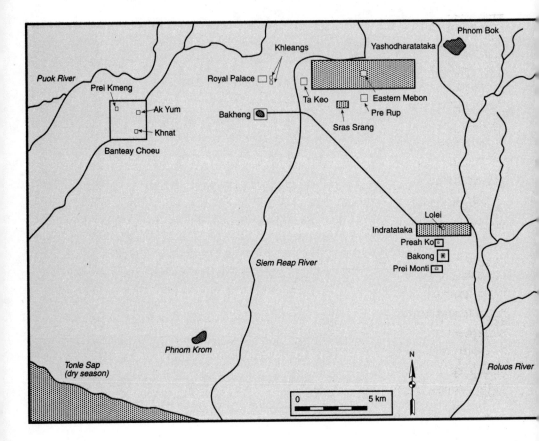

From the reign of Yashovarman, his foundation of Yashodharapura began to take shape. He constructed the Bakheng and Eastern Baray. Rajendravarman was responsible for Pre Rup and the Eastern Mebon, and Jayavarman V built the Ta Keo temple mountain.

66

Royal control of the centre and provinces

The texts of several inscriptions unlock aspects of the administrative and social system, and illuminate the relationship between the centre and the provinces.

Punishment involved the payment of a fine, which diminished with each rung in the social hierarchy. Members of the royal family held the highest rank, followed by royal councillors, dignitaries who had a right to a white parasol with a gold handle, principal traders, votaries of Vishnu and Shiva, and finally the common people.

Some provincial inscriptions relate details of land ownership. A text from Prasat Kuk Pradak in Battambang province, west of the capital, relates how Yashovarman gave five parcels of rice fields at Gamran in the *praman* of Jen Taran to *mratan khlon* Rudraswami when he dedicated a sanctuary. Two years later, Rudraswami petitioned the king to accord him graciously the forest and land of Tamvon in *praman* Purvadisa. A royal order charged *mratan* Vikramayudha, *vyapara* of the second rank, to travel to Purvadisa and meet the local inhabitants. Together, they established the boundaries in order to transfer the land to Rudraswami. He in turn provided betel and coconut trees to the foundation, and banned anyone from calling on those working for the sanctuary to undertake any work other than furnishing water and betel for the fête celebrating the birth of Rama. The king had the authority to allocate land, and a staff of people with the title *vyapara* to establish and fix boundaries. The local dignitary established a temple which, in time-honoured tradition, served an economic role in the accumulation of surpluses. By assigning land in this way, the ruler became intimately involved in the expansion of the area under cultivation, and thereby increased central revenue by way of taxation on production. He also used land grants as a means to reward loyalty.

It is also notable that the kingdom was divided into *praman*. An inscription from Phum Mien may well date to the reign of Yashovarman, but it only mentions a king without naming him.

The brick tower of this temple survives, surrounded by a moat and a large *baray*. The royal order required the *mratan* Sri Vikramasannaha to found a temple in the *praman* of Indrapura. It then lists the property, land, rice fields and workers given exclusively to the foundation. The final lines warn that those transgressing this arrangement will be beheaded.

The royal favour also applied to those living in the centre. A text found within Yashodharapura concerns the royal astrologer, *mratan* Sri Satyasraya, being promoted to the title *mratan khlon* Sri Satyadhipativarman. He erected a statue of Vishnu, to which he offered workers, rice fields and daily measures of rice. Just west of the capital, at Prasat Tasar Sdam, we read of Sri Jayayudha, conqueror of Champa and other countries, who established a temple and made offerings at Lolei of a dwelling, flowers and other riches.

An established state

These texts present a picture of an impressive state. There was a capital centre dominated by the temple housing the royal *linga*. A vast reservoir fed the city moats, and a raised road linked the present with the former capital. The landscape was dotted with new temple foundations. The king headed an administration comprising members of high-status families, many of whom were descended from the pioneer followers of Jayavarman II. The bureaucracy incorporated military leaders, experienced in war against the Chams, as well as priests and those charged with settling land boundaries. This last function highlights the vital relationship between the rural provinces and the centre. The construction programmes of Yashovarman required a large and well-organized labour force. The basic figures reveal that the building of the Bakheng absorbed 8.5 million cubic metres of sandstone. The stone had to be hewn from its source, probably in the Kulen Hills, transported, shaped and put in place. It also needed 4.5 million bricks. The clay had to be dug, moulded and then fired. Numerous trees would have been felled to feed the kilns on an industrial scale. It was necessary to create dykes to retain water in the moats surrounding the city, to dig the canals linking the moats with the *baray* and beyond to the Siem Reap River. The massive dykes that formed Yashodharatataka, the Eastern Baray, comprise over 8 million cubic metres of fill. Then there was the completion of the Indratataka, the building of the Lolei temples, the completion of the linking road between the new and old capitals. *Ashramas* all over the kingdom were built at the king's command.

The key element in this great architectural achievement is the control of labour. Specialist architects, designers, masons and bricklayers had to be housed and sustained. The army of labourers had to be motivated, fed and directed over many years of construction. It may be that the same people who worked on the buildings during the dry season would return to their duties in the rice fields with the rains. This seasonal rhythm endures to this day. The state superstructure, however, fundamentally relied upon agricultural surpluses, a situation that illustrates the importance attached to land tenure and agricultural production.

Yashovarman's sons

This issue is brought sharply into focus in the Tuol Pei inscription from Yashovarman's son and immediate successor, Harshavarman I, dating to AD 922. It includes an order addressed to *mratan* Sri Narendrarimathana concerning a temple foundation for which supplies are guaranteed, because the workers are exempt from other service. Donations included ritual objects, ornaments, animals and rice fields. Most important, it describes an order from Harshavarman to an official with the new title, *rajakulamahamantri*, exempting the foundation from the tax on rice. The Sanskrit word for tax in this context is *vriha*, which probably stems from the word for rice. This text not only informs us about the role of the central administration in an area distant from the capital, but also makes it clear that there was indeed an official in charge of the central taxation system involving rice. It also shows that, since people could be exempted from other

THE CIVILIZATION OF ANGKOR

service, they could be called upon to provide labour in the provinces. Two further inscriptions of this reign also describe royal intervention in provincial matters. A text from Prah Vihear Kuk describes a gift of female workers to a local dignitary, and a second notes the foundation of a hermitage, which received gifts including a pair of buffaloes, two pairs of elephants and workers.

Little else is known of Yashovarman's sons and successors, Harshavarman I and Ishanavarman II. The former probably began the construction of the Baksei Chamkrong temple constructed at Yashodharapura and, as was the tradition with this dynasty, dedicated it to his ancestors Jayavarman III, Indravarman I and his father. This is a modest structure when measured against the Bakheng, but of refined design. The brick shrine is elevated on three tiers of laterite blocks. A contemporary temple, known as Prasat Kravan, was dedicated in AD 921. It comprises five brick towers in a linear arrangement, and the unique interior brick bas-reliefs depict Vishnu.

It was, however, their father Yashovarman who established the first court centre at what is now known as Angkor. His central temple on top of the Bakheng would have stood out from afar as a symbol of his majesty just as the Yashodharatataka, or Eastern Baray, reflected his control of the sacred water flowing from the Kulen upland.

Jayavarman IV

Even while the sons of Yashovarman continued to reign at Yashodharapura, another claimant, Jayavarman IV, established a rival centre to the north-east at Chok Gargyar or Lingapura, whose construction began in AD 921.

Many authorities have described him as a usurper, but the real situation was much more complicated and requires an appreciation of the nature of the succession. Michael Vickery has summarized the basic elements thus: Jayavarman IV was the son of Indravarman's daughter Mahendradevi. He had an elder brother,

Rajendravarman, and a son, Harshavarman II. Jayavarman married his aunt, Jayadevi, who was a half-sister of Yashovarman. He thus inherited a legitimate claim to the throne, which he exercised by founding his own capital. Although it is difficult to sift the truth from the exaggeration, several inscriptions declare that Jayavarman was a man of unusual prowess.

The layout of his court centre at Lingapura followed in the tradition of his grandfather, Indravarman, at Hariharalaya. There was a walled city 1200 metres square, enclosing an inner walled precinct which contained the state temple complex, known as Prasat Thom. This incorporates two walled enclosures, to the east of which lies a large cruciform *gopura*, behind which are two multi-roomed structures sometimes referred to as palaces, but in fact of unknown function. The first major walled enclosure is entered by the Prasat Kraham, and then by a *naga* bridge over the moat. Beyond lie a series of libraries and brick sanctuaries which housed *lingas*. One must cross the moat once more, and pass through a small *gopura*, to approach the enormous principal temple pyramid, raised on seven tiers of descending size traversed by a single stairway. This temple probably housed the image of the *devaraja*, which Jayavarman IV brought to Lingapura. An inscription describes two signatories offering it donations. Beyond the wall of this second enclosure lies a tall mound of unknown function. Immediately to the south-east lies the Rahal *baray*. It measures 1200 × 560 metres, and while not as enormous as the Yashodharatataka of the king's uncle Yashovarman I, it called upon much labour because it had to be partially hewn from living rock. Lingapura is surrounded by a series of subsidiary temples covering an area of 35 square kilometres.

The construction of a new capital during a reign of only two decades must have called upon an army of workers. Fortunately, the builders incorporated many inscriptions in the temples, which provide a glimpse of how that labour was organized and maintained. A series of texts on the western *gopura* of Prasat Krasap, one of the satellite temples at Lingapura, has been described by Aymonier as 'interminable lists of sacred workers'. Despite his jaundiced view of these lists, they represent a shaft of light into the social order of the day, for they provide the names of workers grouped by their place of origin.

We also read of the erection of Tribhuvanesvara, a colossal *linga*, by Jayavarman IV in AD 921. In the same year that the construction of Lingapura began, a *mratan khlon*, Sri Virendradhipativarman, made a donation of workers to the Prasat Kravan.

These inscriptions illustrate that Lingapura was built through the mobilization of labour from many provinces, and taxation in kind, particularly rice, was drafted to sustain them. A similar keen interest in provincial aspects of land tenure and taxation is seen in the few inscriptions of Jayavarman's reign from beyond the capital. A text from Phnom Bayang dating to AD 941, the commencement of the reign of his successor and son Harshavarman II, includes a panegyric for Jayavarman. Set in place by the chief of the *visaya* (territorial area) of Jaranga, the words describe Jayavarman as a great warrior, who ruined his enemy on the field of battle.

An inscription from the same year found at Nong Pang Puey, near Aranyaprathet in Thailand, describes the joining of two foundations, one being dedicated to the god of Lingapura. King Jayavarman was petitioned to combine the personnel of the foundation of *acarya* Paramacarya in *sruk* Vanapura with the royal foundation. A royal order confirmed this, specifying the amount of rice and oil due in payment, and warning that those who disobeyed this order would be caged by the elders of the district and placed before the king for sentence. This area lies 300 kilometres from Lingapura, and the authority of Jayavarman IV, exercised through the high official and brother Rajendravarman, points to the manner in which resources from distant regions were incorporated within the taxation system.

Even a century ago, the sanctity and aura of the Prasat Nan Khmau (which means tower of the black woman) instilled dread into the local people: no official would pass in front of it. A causeway crosses the moat and leads to two brick towers and the foundations of a third. These are in the style of the early tenth century, and were probably built over an earlier foundation. An inscription of AD 928 includes a eulogy to Jayavarman IV, calling him King of Cambodia: 'Fierce in battle, this king's arrows cloud the sky and fill the eyes of his arrogant enemies with the darkness of the night.' A further text from Ampil Rolum also mentions Jayavarman IV as the most blessed of kings, a ruler gifted of unprecedented glory.

The stela from Con An contains an order from the king to link the temple of Jen On with the larger state foundation of Campesvara, with annual dues of rice, butter, eight sets of clothing, 100 cows and ritual vessels. This is one of the few occasions where the modern and Angkorian names for a foundation are the same. The benefactor of the temple provided 117 male and female slaves for the 'dark fortnight', when the moon is waning, and 130 for the period of the waxing moon, each group having one individual in charge.

The majority of Jayavarman's stelae were inscribed in his splendid new capital of Lingapura. The size of the main temple pyramid, the engineering expertise seen in his *baray* and the concentration of sanctuaries speak of a profound commitment of energy. The temple records, set in stone, are at pains to record all the districts of the kingdom called upon to contribute labour and supplies. But other texts, from the far west at Aranyaprathet to the south at Phnom Bayang, record the authority of Jayavarman and present a picture of power and legitimacy, both projected in his building programme, which contradicts the notion of him as a usurper.

Harshavarman II and Rajendravarman I

Jayavarman IV was succeeded by his son Harshavarman II, whose brief tenure at Lingapura was characterized by conflict. An inscription from Prasat Anlon Car in the far south noted that he had in his service one Caitanyashiva, president of his court (*sabhyadhipa*), who founded a monument there.

73

In the byzantine world of dynastic relationships, he was succeeded by a man who was both his uncle and his first cousin, Rajendravarman I. The new king returned the court to Yashodharapura. His two major temple pyramids are located east of the city of Yashovarman. The Eastern Mebon was placed on an island in the middle of the Yashodharatataka, or Eastern Baray, whilst Pre Rup lies to the south.

His accession was not peaceful, if we can believe the inscription set up at Pre Rup. It incorporates a eulogy to Rajendravarman, detailing his illustrious royal ancestry, which was traced back to the mythical founders of Cambodia. Such claims were set out not so much as historic fact, but to reveal his right to the throne. It describes that a king named Puskaraksa was the maternal uncle of the maternal uncle of the mother of Jayavarman II, the king who established his capital on the summit of Mount Mahendra. Jayavarman's mother Mahendradevi, a member of this great line of kings, is portrayed as a goddess, a wife of gods. Rajendravarman himself was a king of kings. His courtiers describe how he frustrated the plans of his enemies. It was a game for him to cut into three a large bar of iron with his sword, hitting it lightly with a single blow as if it were the trunk of a banana tree. His body was hard as diamond. He rent with his sword those who aided the arrogant enemy, reduced them to ashes, and beheaded them. His wars extended to Champa, the region guarded by Indra to the east. Accompanied by his soldiers, who gathered in an army with elephants and horses like a celestial host desiring combat, he advanced to conquer the enemy. The inscription contains many vivid descriptions of the king in battle, his sword red with the blood of his foes. In redoubled fits of hyperbole, we read of the glory of this king, who punished the guilty but had an ocean of compassion for the innocent, a king who shone like the full moon.

As with his predecessors, the state temple of Pre Rup was designed to honour the king and his ancestors within the context of the god Shiva. It is of harmonious design, its five major towers rising on two laterite tiers. When covered in stucco and doubtless painted, it would have dominated the new capital of which it probably formed the centre. The largest and centrally placed brick sanctuary housed Rajendrabhadresvara, the royal *linga*. The four subsidiary towers were dedicated first to Isvara Rajendravarmesvara, representing the king; to Rajendravesvarupa, in favour of the Brahman Vishvarupa, a distant ancestor of the king; to Rajendravarman's aunt Jayadevi; and to his predecessor Harshavarman II. The temple also housed numerous subsidiary shrines, libraries and *gopuras* incorporating two walled precincts.

King Rajendravarman had already ordered the architect Kavindrarimathana to design a slightly smaller but very similar temple on an island in the centre of the Yashodharatataka, to promote himself and his ancestors. The central tower held a *linga* named Rajendresvara, and the four subsidiary temples on the uppermost platform housed images of the king's forebears. Access from the *baray* was by four sets of steps leading up to a terrace. The outer wall was pierced in front of each set by a cruciform *gopura* and the visitor then reached a platform divided by long rows of galleries. A flight of steps then led up to a further terrace containing brick towers and laterite structures, leading after a further set of steps flanked by stone lions to the upper five towers. Rajendravarman's reign also saw the completion of the sanctuary of Baksei Chamkrong, dedicated by a golden statue to Shiva, and two Buddhist temples south of the Yashodharatataka.

The construction of the new capital just east of Yashodharapura is but one aspect of Rajendravarman's kingdom. The inscriptions on rural monuments provide the counterbalance: how was society as a whole structured? As far as can be judged by the distribution of these texts, the rule of Rajendravarman extended over the same area as his predecessors Yashovarman I and Jayavarman IV. This incorporated the area north of the Tonle Sap, east towards Sisophon, and the valley of the Mekong from Phnom Penh to the upper delta. There may have been an intensification of settlement in the premier rice-growing region of Battambang. Most temple texts follow the established procedure of extolling the virtues of the monarch, but their primary intention was to record meritorious acts including the purchase and endowment of land, the ownership of rice fields, the demarcation of boundaries and the duties of workers. In the case of disputes, the subordination of provincial to state temples, or the management of royal assets, we can also perceive the bureaucracy at work. Most inscriptions end with the warning of dire consequences for those who steal or violate foundation property, a sure indication that thievery flourished.

The relationship between the centre and the provinces is seen in an inscription from the far south at Ba Phnom. After the traditional eulogy to the king, it lists honours bestowed on a *mantrin*, Mahendradhipativarman, which included a golden litter, a white parasol and a parasol with peacock feathers. His daughter Narendradevi was a consort of King Rajendravarman. Although damage to a vital part of the text obscures details, it lists many foundations and offerings probably endowed by Mahendradhipativarman, including a Vishnu image at Yashodharapura. He transformed forested land into a village, and at Gajapura, he consecrated an image and made a *baray*. At Purandarapura, he extended an existing *baray* and had a brick shrine built north of the abode of Vishnu. 'In a place of pasture where water was difficult to obtain, in a forested hollow, he made a reservoir fed by three rivers, as was the proper thing to do, for the benefit of others.' Here, we see a local grandee linked to the court by his daughter's relationship with the king, making merit by founding religious institutions in conjunction with forest clearance and the provision of reservoirs. The Khmer text describes the boundaries of rice fields, which include, at Ransi Gval, all the ponds to the east and to the south as far as the canal; and to the north as far as the canal at Panlin. Cœdès has suggested that the word used for canal in this section implies use in irrigation. Moreover, many of the boundaries for rice fields are described as reservoirs.

We can gain further insight into rural organization in an inscription from Kdei Skie. After a eulogy of the king's renown in battle, the author describes how he raised images of Vishnu and

Lakshmi. The inscription then set out the boundaries of the gods' land: to the north, the channel leading to Subhava; to the south, to the lane that comes from Madhavapura; and to the west, just to the north-east angle of the basin of Gamryan; then to the brick-works. The word channel as part of a rice field boundary again hints at the distribution of water.

Still far from the capital, an inscription from Basak describes how the king defeated his enemies and then restored damaged buildings at Yashodharapura. Then it refers to the construction of the Eastern Mebon, or island temple, on the Yashodhara lake, with its five towers covered in stucco. The king's devoted servant, *mratan* Sri Nrpendrayudha, was granted a litter. He made gifts of gold, silver and other metals, elephants, buffaloes, cattle, horses, workers, villages, rice fields, land revenues and other goods to the god who is named, in the Khmer text, Nrpendrayudhasvami.

Rice is most commonly listed among dues paid to the rural foundations, but another text from Basak tells how Rajendravar-man gave an edict to his *vrah guru* with rules for the provision of holy oil, in the form of butter, collected for the royal treasury and other users. It nominated four persons to be responsible for col-lecting the oil, which was destined for temple rituals, and in cases of failure to do so, the fine was a pair of cattle. Fifteen men and women were nominated to safeguard the sacred herd for each half of the month, and to ensure that the animals were properly stabled and their quarters maintained. The division of labour by rota into two groups on the basis of a waxing or waning moon sug-gests that half an individual's time was required for serving the foundation.

The same relationship between land and temple foundations is seen in the northern part of the state where, at Prasat Thnal Chuk, the text of an inscription describes an order from Rajendravarman to the *kamsten an Rajakulamahamantri* and three *mratans*. This complex of seven brick buildings is surround-ed by a wall 32 × 26 metres on all but the west side. The simple entrance in the eastern wall leads to two galleries and three shrines in the centre, beyond which lie two smaller structures.

We read of the owner, Pancagavya, and his donations to the foundation of Santipada of slaves, animals and rice fields, together with the daily supply of rice to the god at the state temple of Lingapura. The names of male and female workers with their children for the light and dark days of the month are set out, followed by a listing of 100 cattle, 20 buffaloes, 'the rice fields to produce the god's rice' situated to the south of the basin next to the river, and 'the rice field where one grows the rice for the god of Lingapura'.

War and its aftermath are recorded in an inscription from the northern enclosure at Ishanapura, the old capital of Ishanavarman, where on his return from a campaign in Champa a warrior called Vikramasingha gave his property to the king and founded several sanctuaries with endowments of land and workers. He was one of a line of aristocrats, for his father was a member of Yashovarman's court and his grandfather was named Virendravarman. He also restored the local cult to the god Gambhiresvara.

Kuk Sla Ket is a group of sanctuaries just west of Yashodharapura, founded by a family of royal retainers of which the latest, Ksetrajna, was appointed barber to Rajendravarman and given the title *mahendropakalpa*. Its inscription first provides his list of the kings from Indravarman I to the present and their relationships, and then enumerates his own family line and their service to successive kings. Two brothers served Jayavarman III and Indravarman, and their nephew served Yashovarman I. Ksetrajna himself, in recognition of his duties, was given a white parasol and a gold cordon. He placed an image of Vishnu in the central shrine and had two others built alongside, south and north.

Tuk Cum (surrounded by water) lies just east of the great stone bridge which carries the Angkorian road west from Angkor over the Stung Sreng. There is a brick sanctuary here, surrounded by a small moat. In AD 949, Bajrendracarya and his nephew, *vap* Dhu, erected a statue there as an act of merit. They assigned workers, villages, rice fields and plantations to the foundation. Their inscription describes how they acquired further rice fields. For example, they paid for them in oxen, ivory and cloth, set in place the boundaries and offered the fields to their foundation. Workers assigned to the temple are listed. For the light fifteen days of the month, there were two cooks, a leaf sewer, a perfume grinder and rice for the god. This text does not mention any form of royal assent.

The relationship between the workers and the foundation to which they were tied is clarified by an inscription found on a monolith of a cave in Phnom Kanva, Battambang. It describes how a male worker called Viruna, born on the sacred domain, escaped from it and after being captured had his eyes gouged out and his nose removed. The wretch and his family were reassigned exclusively to the sanctuary.

Jayavarman V

Rajendravarman was succeeded by his ten-year-old son, Jayavarman V, in AD 968. In his youth, the state had to call on aristocratic officials to hold the reins of government. Several emerge from the inscriptions as the founders of temples and owners of estates. Government continued to be based at Yashodharapura, but the king maintained the tradition of having his own state temple, and we learn that it was under construction by the time he was aged seventeen. It was known then as Hemasringagiri, the mountain with the golden summits, but today has the less mellifluous name of Ta Keo. Built to represent Mount Meru, the home of the gods, it is located just west of the Yashodharatataka. Like Pre Rup, it comprises five sanctuaries built on the uppermost level of a tiered pyramid, surrounded by two walled enclosures and a moat. It seems likely that the entire structure was due to be decorated, but it remains unfinished. A high royal official, Yogisvarapandita, described how a thunder-bolt, perhaps a lightning strike, hit the building. He undertook a ceremony to expiate this evil omen and bought stones and elephants to complete the monument, but without success. Hemasringagiri was linked by a causeway to a landing stage in the centre of the west bank of the Yashodharatataka, and it was in this area that Jacques preferred to place the royal palace of Jayavarman V which, with the state temple to the south, was known as Jayendranagari, or the capital of the victorious king.

The wealth of the elite court families is best appreciated at the temple of Banteay Srei, 25 kilometres north-east of Jayendranagari. This delightful temple in pink sandstone was founded by Yajnyavaraha, a grandson of King Harshavarman I who served as one of Rajendravarman's ministers and then became teacher and adviser to Jayavarman V. The foundation stela names Yajnyavaraha and his brother Vishnukumara as grandsons of Harshavarman, and the temple was consecrated on 22 April 967. We read that Yajnavaraha was a scholar and philanthropist who helped those suffering from illness, injustice or poverty. Daily, they came to his house, the wretched, the abandoned, the feeble, old or young, seeking help. As acts of merit, he founded many monasteries, setting in place statues of Shiva and having reservoirs constructed. The king honoured him with parasols of peacock feathers, golden palanquins and other insignia of high esteem and status. A text from Banteay Srei, dating from early in the reign of Jayavarman V, sets out some of the donations for functionaries of the temple, which include white rice. The inscription also established the boundaries of the estates designated to endow it. Vittorio Roveda has suggested that the wall of the first enclosure and its western entrance portal are the only parts of the original temple to be seen today. Its sanctity, however, may be judged from the many later additions which have produced its present form.

Jayavarman's inscriptions concentrate in the good agricultural lands to the north and west of the Tonle Sap, east to the Mekong River and then south towards the upper delta. They illuminate aspects of the legal and administrative system, but also reveal an image of the landscape and rural life. It is evident that both the king and the great aristocratic families owned extensive estates. Indralakshmi, for example, the younger sister of the king, married Divakara, who is said to have come from India. They probably

This rich male burial from Noen U-Loke reveals how prehistoric societies were growing increasingly complex as we approach the transition to statehood in Southeast Asia.

Burial 113, a rich woman from Noen U-Loke, incorporated fine ceramic vessels, bronzes, and a necklace of gold and agate beads.

The temples in Group C at Ishanapura were accompanied
by water basins lined in laterite.

Banteay Prei Nokor was quite possibly an early capital of King Jayavarman II.
The walls on the horizon give an impression of its massive size.

ABOVE: Two brick shrines dominate the centre of Banteay Prei Nokor.

RIGHT: The brick temple of Lolei was once covered in painted stucco. Traces survive to reveal how ornate it was when completed by Yasovarman.

ABOVE: The temple of Preah Ko, the sacred ox, contains shrines dedicated
to Rudravarman and Prithivindradevi, respectively Indravarman's maternal
grandfather and father, with the central tower being dedicated to Jayavarman II.
Each royal ancestor's name was joined to that of Shiva, thus projecting the
image of deified ancestors. The three sanctuaries in the second row
acknowledged the principal consorts of each lord.

RIGHT: Phnom Chisor was one of the great temples of the Angkorian state.
This view from the summit looks south to the long flight of access steps,
the gopura and baray.

LEFT: The Phimeanakas was the chapel royal of the kings of Angkor and occupied a central position within the walled precinct of the royal palace. Ringed by water basins and covered in gold, it must have impressed all who saw it.

BELOW: Prasat Kravan was dedicated in 921 AD. It comprises five brick towers in a linear arrangement, and the unique interior brick bas reliefs depict Vishnu.

Even under reconstruction, the Baphuon is one of the most impressive of Angkorian temple pyramids. Built by Udayadityavarman II, this monument is embellished with fine bas reliefs. An inscription from Lovek calls it the tower of gold, and it was described by Zhou Daguan as the tower of copper, taller even than the neighbouring Bayon.

A princess is borne aloft on her palanquin in the train of King Suryavarman. The reliefs of Angkor Wat are a unique source of information on the court under his reign.

Angkor Wat was the temple and mausoleum of the Vishnuite King Suryavarman II. It is the largest religious edifice known. Antonio de Magdalena described it to Diogo de Couto in these terms: 'Half a league from this city is a temple called Angar. It is of such extraordinary construction that it is not possible to describe it with a pen, particularly since it is like no other building in the world. It has towers and decoration and all the refinements which the human genius can conceive of.'

The lotus towers of Angkor Wat rise above the forest. How much more impressive would this view from the summit of the Bakheng have been when the towers were sheathed in gold.

Apsaras, or celestial dancers, were carved at Angkor Wat to ensure that the deified king was suitably accompanied on his arrival in paradise.

The central shrine of Angkor Wat rises inexorably to the central lotus tower.

The moat surrounding Angkor Wat is a major engineering feat.

The first image of a king of Angkor shows Suryavarman in state. It was he who inspired Angkor Wat as his temple and mausoleum. He sits on this throne, surrounded by fans, parasols and fly whisks.

Early Portuguese visitors described this stone city lost in the jungle. The grandeur of this, the southern entrance to Jayavarman's city of Angkor Thom, continues to amaze.

Zhou Daguan in 1296 noted that, 'to the east, a golden bridge flanked by gilded lions gave way to a pavilion supported by stone elephants'. This was the elephant terrace, a great viewing stand linked to the royal palace. Note the central tower of the Bayon rising above the trees in the distance.

A rare scene from the Bayon shows a family following the army on the march.

Jayavarman VII laced his kingdom with roads, bridges and rest houses for travellers. Here is his magnificent bridge over the Chikreng River.

Servants prepare food and fill containers for a feast in the forest. A bas relief from the Bayon.

The enemy attacked the Khmer on the Great Lake. The Chams carry curiously-shaped crescentic shields and have elaborate head dresses. Their highly-decorated galleys are propelled by oarsmen.

A game of chess absorbs the attention of the players in a quiet corner at the Bayon.

The bas reliefs of the Bayon temple portray many aspects of daily life at Angkor. Here, a woman in childbirth is being attended by three midwives as she lies under the shade of a wooden pavilion.

The Bayon temple, Madhyadri, lies in the centre of Angkor Thom. The giant heads on the temple towers have been seen as representations of the king as a boddhisattva.

Two men prepare to release their fighting boars.

lived at a place called Dvijendrapura, a few kilometres south of Jayendranagari, where their inscriptions have been found in the ruined foundations of a sanctuary. These temples contained images of Vishnu and the princess's mother, and it lists the ornaments associated with statues of each: ear pendants, crowns, bracelets and precious stones. A list of foundation property cites a golden palanquin gifted by the king in AD 968, silver bowls, parasols with golden handles, silver libation vessels and a mirror. It then records 171 male and female slaves and their children. We also learn of the estates donated to the foundation. One was the subject of a dispute over ownership, which called on royal intervention to settle the issue through mediation involving two officials with the title *khlon glan* (chief of the warehouse) of the second and third rank. The boundaries were fixed after consultation with, among others, the old people of the area and were described as a royal donation to the foundation. In a significant passage, the text distinguishes rice fields next to the river from dry season rice fields.

The same couple placed a similar inscription at their extensive property of Prasat Komphus. This site comprises the remains of five brick sanctuaries, a surrounding wall, two libraries, a large moat and *gopuras*, beyond which lie more foundations and *barays*. The main inscription describes foundations of Divakara in the Madhuvana 'honey forest', and lays down the amount of rice required to maintain the endowment, together with a monthly measure of honey. It also lists the ornaments donated for the god, for the Shiva *linga*, and for the images of Indralakshmi and the mother of Rajendravarman. Other valuables include parasols with golden handles, silver fly whisks and fans of peacock feathers. A number of officials, including a chief of corvée labour (*khlon karya*), learned men, inspectors of quality and defaults, and chiefs of the warehouses, all received a palanquin by royal favour, while prosperity is assured to the ascetics attached to the gods of this place.

In 979, the king addressed his *vrah guru* and high officials with an instruction to offer land to four highly ranked princes, *kamsten*

Sri Rajapativarman (brother-in-law to the king), Narapativaravarman (Rajendravarman's maternal nephew), *mratan khlon* Sri Jayayudhavarman (brother of Narapativaravarman), and an unnamed person who was probably the queen. The princes set up an inscription at Prasat Char, a rich foundation of three shrines with two surrounding walls. It declares that they will found settlements, raise temples and provide accommodation for their families. It gives the limit of their land. An enclave owned by *vap* Vis was obtained by exchange with another piece of land. It then gives a listing of other lands obtained by royal order as well as land graciously given by the king. One parcel of this block was reserved for herds, another for the slaves who furnished oil for Lingapura. There are some arresting details of rural life. *Mratan* Hrdayabhava, guardian of the bedchamber, third category, killed two elephants belonging to the *kamsten*, which were eating his rice. He had no elephants himself to compensate the *kamsten* for the loss, so gave up some land.

When the king had reached the age of sixteen in 974, he took part in a ceremony 'by the sacred stone basin', in which he founded two religious corporations that could hold land, had inheritance rights and were exempt from taxes. His high official, known as the *vrah guru*, was required to select twenty individuals as foundation members of each corporate group. He also had to ensure that the statutes be engraved on gold and silver leaves and placed in the court of justice. The founder members were presented with flowers. The stelae recording this act of royal merit defined the land endowed to the foundations in considerable detail. Members had exclusive rights to the revenues of the enfeoffed communities and workers, and were exempt from taxes on rice and oil. Strict regulations were put in place lest the former leaders in their respective areas attempted to reclaim their property or transgress the corporations' rights. Priests who distinguished themselves by their learning were appointed to the court as teachers.

Most foundations remained in the traditional Hindu canon. A text from Phnom Mrec (or pepper hill) in a district called Gamryan describes how Soma gave an endowment of land to a sanctuary of Shiva. His two brick shrines lie today on the side of the hill commanding a view of the flat rice fields to the east, from which he could have doubtless seen the field boundaries, which included the bank of the basin and the main route to the west. It is intriguing to note the price he paid for a piece of land: two pairs of buffaloes and four *jyan* of silver. For a second parcel, he paid two slaves, a measure of gold, a pair of buffaloes and two cattle 'to drive a team quickly'. A third parcel of land was graciously offered by the king to the foundation, whilst the regulations noted that the foundation was exempt from royal service and from the tax on oil. The prices paid for slaves assigned to the temple of the goddess Bhagabati are set out in an inscription from Phum Mien. Several were exchanged for other slaves, and one was bought from a Vietnamese for silver. Further to the south at Basak, we read of a royal edict that a piece of land with a long history of royal ownership be endowed to the god at Vak Ek with a daily offering of rice, lighting oil and oil of sacred cows, together with slaves. Several officials comprised a committee to oversee the endowment of the land, and *mratan* Sri Narendrasimha, *senapati* (general) of the front gate, was ordered to place the boundary markers of this territory and to erect an inscribed stela at Vak Ek giving exclusive rights over this land to the temple.

The dynasty of Jayavarman II: royal power and social organization

When Jayavarman V established his court in successive centres between the Tonle Sap and the Kulen Hills, he brought with him many followers. According to inscriptions set in place two centuries or more later, the heads of these families occupied important religious and lay roles in the king's system of government and were rewarded with land grants. We thus trace the names of the hereditary fan carriers to thirteen successive rulers or to the chief priests of the *devaraja* cult. The succession within these aristocratic families passed through the female line, from the head of the family to his sister's son. The trend towards centralized authority, identified in the administration of Jayavarman I of Chenla, was greatly strengthened by Jayavarman II and his successors. The central court was the heart of the social system. At least from the reign of Indravarman I and probably from that of Jayavarman II, this comprised a temple dedicated to the king and his ancestors, combined with Shiva. There would be a royal palace and, except in ephemeral reigns, a reservoir. The central temple would be enclosed by walls and often by a moat. As the palaces were built of wood, their layout is unknown, and extensive excavations are necessary to illuminate the urban landscape. Representations of wooden palaces on temple walls, however, reveal the rich secular architectural tradition that has not survived.

Successive rulers established their own court centres. During the reign of Jayavarman II, courts were established at Amarendrapura, Hariharalaya and Mahendraparvata. Indravarman I ruled at Hariharalaya, Yashovarman at Yashodharapura, Jayavarman IV at Lingapura, Rajendravarman at old Yashodharapura, but at a location to the east of his predecessor, and Jayavarman V at Jayendrapura, again slightly removed from his father's court.

The extent of the kingdom

The distribution of inscriptions gives us some idea of the extent of successive kingdoms, how central government worked and the means whereby the court was sustained. The kingdom encompassed the riverine and lacustrine lowlands of Cambodia, with particular focus on the area north of the Tonle Sap and the valley of the Mekong River. There is little or no evidence for any form of Angkorian political control either in the west, in the Chao Phraya Valley or in the broad ricelands of the Mun Valley to the north. The administrative apparatus to control the kingdom involved a central bureaucracy and a corps of loyal regional officials. The former called upon members of the elite aristocratic families, many of whom traced their ancestry to the followers of

Jayavarman II and were often related to the royal line by family ties.

There was an administrative hierarchy, identified through titles, grades and insignia, which over time evolved in complexity and in the range of duties. A high official named Sri Nivasakavi served as the *hotar* to Jayavarman III and Indravarman. An inscription from the Bakong temple at Hariharalaya praises his many virtues, knowledge and religious dedication. A text from Prasat Kandol Dom, adjacent to Preah Ko, describes a second official, Shivasoma, as the king's guru. He was the grandson of a king named Jayendradhipativarman, who was in turn the maternal uncle of Jayavarman II. Shivasoma was thus first cousin once removed of Jayavarman II. As members of the royal line ramified and served in the court, so there developed an increasingly large group of aristocratic retainers from which to appoint functionaries. Indravarman I also appointed Amarabhava as a chief of religious foundations. He had a reservoir constructed for the members of a foundation because water was difficult to obtain, and was honoured by Yashovarman I with the title *acaryadhipati*, or head *acarya*.

New court titles and duties

Two senior figures subsequently occupied positions of the highest authority under the king, the *rajakulamahamantri* and the *vrah guru*.

The former appears first in a text dating to the reign of Harshavarman I. Several inscriptions show this person's responsibility for issuing tax immunity for religious institutions and permission for the joining of foundations. We also see him exercising his authority in the sacred court, with powers to punish those who transgressed a royal edict.

The *vrah guru* discharged both ritual and civil duties. We find him, for example, fulfilling rituals to ensure wet season rains, transmitting royal edicts to various foundations and playing a role in the foundation of two religious corporations.

The number of officials increased markedly during the reign of Rajendravarman and again during that of Jayavarman V. The central court included functionaries of various degrees of rank, charged with authority over the royal warehouses, or the proper surveying of land boundaries. Courtiers also served the king personally, as fan bearers, holders of fly whisks, pages of the bedchamber and as doctors. Although not given prominence in the inscriptions, the energy expended upon temple construction and provision of water makes it clear that court centres incorporated architects, designers, a host of skilled artisans and access to a large labour force. During these last two reigns, the leading aristocratic families increased their wealth to the point that they were able to found and endow substantial religious foundations, as at Banteay Srei. This trend had political implications at the death of Jayavarman V, when the succession was disputed.

Beyond the capital: control in the provinces

The court centre represents the apex of the social pyramid, but its very existence turned upon the control and organization of the sustaining area: the countryside. Almost all the written records survive because they were inscribed on stone. The archives of the court and provinces, being made of perishable materials, remain lost to us although an inscription from Tuol Prasat refers to Sahadeva, librarian of the sacred records.

The establishment by the centre of political control over the sustaining territory and its people is a key issue in the development of states. The inscriptions reveal a significant development, for they employ first the term *praman*, and then *visaya*, to describe large territorial divisions. New names, such as Purvadisa and Sanduk, emerge for these units, which were linked with the names of individuals bearing the title *khlon visaya*. Their duties included the definition of land boundaries and doubtless the maintenance of records of ownership. They witnessed land transactions, placed boundary markers and, on occasion, made meritorious donations to religious foundations. The latter institutions, and those identified for specific payments in kind to the central authority, fell outside their jurisdiction.

We also encounter the *tamrvac*, who appear to have been centrally appointed agents for the government in the provinces, essential intermediaries for overseeing royal edicts. It is possible that some villages within a *visaya* were grouped for administrative purposes in a unit intermediate in size between a community and a province, but the village itself, then as now, was the heart of the agricultural system. We read of a *khlon sruk* as being an individual responsible for village matters, aided by the old people in cases where land ownership was in question, or criminals had to be handed over to higher authorities. This system of rule had, as its central duty, the proper collection of payments in kind to sustain the court centre and its bureaucracy. Taxation centred upon surplus products. The state of Angkor never employed a monetary system although measures of gold and silver are commonly mentioned as media used in trade transactions.

The legal system

Theft and trespass must have been encountered often, to judge from the regular warning against both and the dire consequences for the guilty. Since these texts are the sole source of our information on the judicial system and they treat issues of land ownership and transfer, most of our information on crime and punishment stems from land disputes. The ritual eulogies of royalty indicate that the king stood at the apex of the legal system, but we also read of the sacred court and of high officials becoming involved in litigation.

An inscription from Tuol Prasat dating to the reign of Jayavarman V describes a legal dispute involving land tenure. This text reveals how landed estates were passed down through generations of the same family, albeit at the risk of false claims or expropriation. Sahadeva, the rightful owner, describes how his property was obtained by his maternal great-grandfather Gavya, a man of wealth, generosity and wisdom, who observed the law. Ownership of the land and the village of Devigrama had been confirmed by King Rajendravarman, who had ordered that boundaries be established. At that point, Gavya had raised an image to a deity and organized the construction of water basins. On his death, the land was claimed by three men, named Hi, Pu and Ke, the last-named being a kinsman of Sahadeva. The property markers placed by royal order were ripped out, and Sahadeva, the descendant of Gavya, informed the king in writing of these crimes. King Jayavarman V ordered a detailed enquiry by his ministers, resulting in the condemnation of Pu and his gang. When they were declared guilty, the court ordered that their lips and hands be cut off. There must have been serious disputes within the same family over ownership because new claims then arose, which occurred just after the death of Jayavarman V. Again the claimants were punished following a court enquiry, and on this occasion, their feet and heads were crushed.

A second text dating from the reign of Jayavarman V reveals that legal enquiries could also safeguard the interests of an injured party. On this occasion, part of the land donated to a god by *vap* Dharma was claimed by a woman, who removed the new boundary markers. An enquiry revealed that she had acted within her rights and had relocated the new boundaries to take account of her property.

These disputes indicate how the landed class could seek legal intervention, but we know little of the rights, if any, of the people whom the inscriptions describe as slaves, who could be bought for silver, or exchanged one with the other. On one occasion such a person escaped and was mutilated on recapture. We do know, however, that witnesses in court proceedings came from all levels of society. An edict of Yashovarman declared that punishment for infringing temple regulations was graded according to the rank of the offender. At the apex of the social scale, royal princes were fined twenty *pala* of gold. *Mantrin* paid half this amount; those with the right to a white parasol with a gold handle half as much again; but common people might suffer a hundred lashes. Despite such gaps in our understanding, there is no doubt that the law was effective in resolving disputes and meting out punishment in areas remote from the court centre.

The dynasty of Jayavarman II: conclusions

Jayavarman II and his successors ruled a state that relied, in the final analysis, upon the production of a rice surplus. In all the transactions recorded, none mentions a formal system of currency, although measures of silver or gold were employed. The inscriptions rather reveal an intense concern with the quality of agricultural land, and the details of ownership and boundaries. There were many officials whose responsibility was to assess and collect dues. Whilst rice was the key, other products are also mentioned: wax, oil, honey, salt and cloth. The state also required labour, organized at ground level by the official known as a *khlon karya*.

In terms of infrastructure, the rivers linking outlying areas to the centre via the Tonle Sap must have been instrumental in transporting goods to the court. The owners of landed estates seem to have controlled the labour of villagers on their land, and there are many references to the construction of reservoirs. The degree to which these were used in rice agriculture is not known, but we read on occasion of channels issuing from them. If present customs are a guide, they would have had multiple benefits, not least the provision of water for local communities during the months of the dry season.

The production of economic surpluses was but one strand, albeit vital, in the body politic. Religion was equally important in meshing together and unifying members of society. A raised temple pyramid, incorporating shrines to Shiva, the king and his ancestors, lay at the physical centre of the state. Objects of devotion began with the *linga* whose name combined that of the king of the gods with that of the king on earth. The founding inscriptions of the state temples laid down the lineage of the sovereign as his right to rule. In the countryside, numerous other temples were the foci of local communities. These were commonly founded by aristocrats with endowments of land and labour. Such religious foundations were usually exempt from the taxation system, and called on their own tied labour for sustenance. Their contribution to the realm was vital, if intangible, for the king shared a proportion of the merit accumulated by those making the endowment.

Jayavarman V was the last major king of a dynasty which, for two centuries, had established a state centred north of the Tonle Sap, with a sustaining area that incorporated lowlands converted to rice fields and was veined by a river system with the Mekong as its main line of communication. His death in about AD 1000 was followed by civil war and a new dynasty, founded by King Suryavarman I.

CHAPTER 6

THE DYNASTY OF THE SUN KINGS:
AD 1000–1080

In 1011, about five years after his arrival at the capital of Yashodharapura, a new king, Suryavarman I, summoned his officials to swear an oath of allegiance. Many *tamrvac* of the first to fourth ranks offered their lives and unswerving devotion to the king in the presence of the sacred fire. It signalled the end of a period of civil war over who should succeed Jayavarman V, and the re-establishment of a regime in which the central court was the hub of a kingdom sustained by the loyalty and estates of the great landed families. The officials promised to safeguard the meritorious foundations of the country and urged the king to punish severely those who supported any rival.

But who was this new king? Suryavarman's origins and legitimacy have spawned many theories, even including a distant origin in Malaysia. More recently, Michael Vickery has suggested looking at thirteen lengthy inscriptions which set out the dynastic histories of the aristocratic families of the preceding two centuries. These texts were carved in stone following serious disputes over the succession and civil strife. Some of the statements made are patently false. There are two claims that some families' lineages all served the same king in the same capacity, while four state that their particular ancestor was the *rajapurohita*, or royal chaplain, to Jayavarman II. Most of these lineages trace their origins to the followers of Jayavarman II, and some note intermarriage with members of the royal family, showing how a growing number of elite families filled

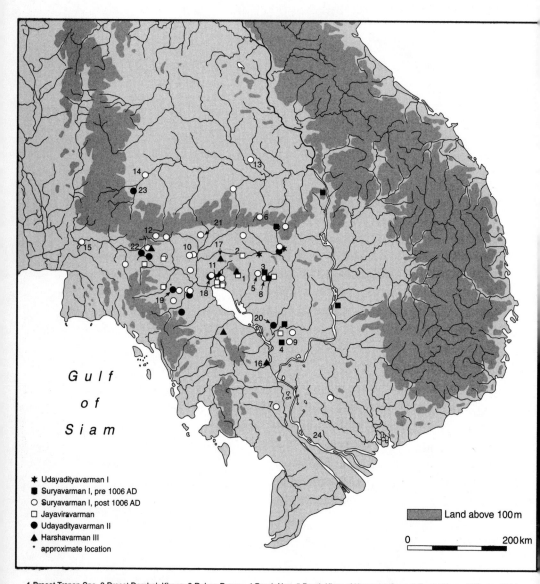

Gulf

of

Siam

✷ Udayadityavarman I
■ Suryavarman I, pre 1006 AD
○ Suryavarman I, post 1006 AD
□ Jayaviravarman
● Udayadityavarman II
▲ Harshavarman III
* approximate location

Land above 100 m

0   200 km

1 Prasat Trapan Sno, 2 Prasat Dambok Khpos, 3 Roban Romas, 4 Preah Nan, 5 Preah Khan of Kompong Svay, 6 Preah Vihear, 7 Phnom Chisor, 8 Prasat Trapan Run, 9 Kuk Prin Crum, 10 Nak Ta Cih Ko, 11 Wat Prah That de Tuk Cha, 12 Phnom Sanke Kon, 13 Ban Khamoy, 14 Phimai, 15 Prachinburi, 16 Lonvek, 17 Prasat Prah Khset, 18 Vrah Damnap, 19 Baset, 20 Phum Da, 21 Prasat Ta Kham Thom, 22 Sdok Kak Thom, 23 Phnom Wan, 24 The Plain of Reeds

The distribution of inscriptions of the dynasty of the Sun Kings.

central court functions. In an atmosphere of uncertainty, particularly for those who backed the wrong faction in a civil war, it was clearly wise to advertise a long, loyal and noble ancestry, even if some of these claims were false.

One inscription establishes the aristocratic lineage of the Saptadevakula family, whose members claimed descent from the probable maternal grandfather of Indravarman I and held the title of chief of the fan carriers. They traced back their noble origins earlier than the reign of Jayavarman II. If Suryavarman, as seems likely, belonged to this line of descent, then his faction could have claimed legitimacy. To support this, Vickery points out that Suryavarman's predecessor and successor were both named Udayadityavarman. Thus all three bore names incorporating either the Sanskrit word for the sun (surya) or the rising sun (aditya). The first of Udayadityavarman's inscriptions comes from the same north-eastern area as the early texts of Suryavarman. Although there are no clear statements on their relationship, the sun image included in their names suggests a unity that encourages their dynasty to be named 'The Dynasty of the Sun Kings'.

But Suryavarman's path to the throne had not been easy. Following the death of Jayavarman V, two other rulers also sought the throne: Udayadityavarman I and Jayaviravarman.

Udayadityavarman I's mother was a sister of a wife of Jayavarman V. This provided only the faintest claim to legitimacy. One text shows him confirming temple rights to indented labour, but reserving the right to call on workers if necessary. Both texts come from sites located north-east of the capital, Yashodharapura, yet the new king probably resided in the palace of Jayavarman V.

This is the last we hear of him, for both at the capital and to the west, we encounter inscriptions that mention a second king, Jayaviravarman, a ruler whose claims to legitimacy are unknown. Administrative continuity from the previous regime in the areas he controlled is reflected in some of his texts. For example, one requests that he allow the people of Divapura to enter the corporation of goldsmiths as artisans. But another rival was already on the march.

A series of contemporary inscriptions from east or north-east of the capital, though lacking the eulogies due to a sovereign, mention Suryavarman as a ruler who exercised the prerogatives of kingship. In a text from Roban Romas dated to AD 1001, for example, we find that the property donated by Sri Somesvarapandita of *sruk* Jen Suren to a new foundation included land given by Suryavarman. At Preah Nan in AD 1002, Sri Prithivindrapandita of *sruk* Ay Ramani offered a sanctuary foundation to Suryavarman with endowments and payments of rice, cow dung, land, silver, mustard and beans. Clearly Suryavarman was consolidating his hold on territory.

However, north-east of Yashodharapura, contemporary inscriptions of Jayaviravarman describe boundary disputes and suggest conflict. In AD 1003, an order was issued to replace boundaries that had been uprooted and destroyed at Prasat Trapan Sno. Two years later at Prasat Dambok Khpos, in the shadow of the Kulen plateau, someone incised on the door jamb a demand to seize and impale those who had destroyed boundary markers.

But by 1006, Suryavarman appears to have been in authority at the capital. Sri Tapasvisvarapandita recorded, on a building known as the Northern Khleang, that he had made a foundation and offered the merit to Suryavarman, who made gifts in return. No more is heard of Jayaviravarman after this date.

The price to be paid for Suryavarman's victory and the establishment of his dynasty is found in the Sdok Kak Thom inscription. This records in great detail the history of a noble family from the reign of Jayavarman II, and describes the devastation caused by civil war and the need to restore, rebuild and re-endow foundations and estates.

Suryavarman, the builder and restorer

The construction of temples, reservoirs and, doubtless, palaces of unprecedented splendour was a means of displaying royal status and grandeur. Suryavarman was no exception; indeed, he seems to have seized this initiative as a means of consolidating his hold on power. It is probable that even before his arrival at Yashodharapura, he initiated a massive project at Preah Khan of Kompong Svay, 75 kilometres to the east. First reported by Louis Delaporte in 1873, the full extent of this huge centre was only realized following an aerial photographic survey in 1937, when the exterior walls and moats were traced. These revealed a square almost 5 kilometres on each side, the eastern walls being punctured by a *baray* 2.8 kilometres long and 750 metres wide. The interior further reveals two walled enclosures culminating in the central shrine. One of the problems in ascribing this most impressive site to Suryavarman during his early years east of Angkor is that some shrines belong to a later period. However, an inscription from the second enclosure records his presence, and some architectural design features belong to his reign. Further archaeological research is needed to unravel the history of this site, but there can be little doubt that its early history was set in the period of Suryavarman's campaign for supremacy.

Peace also brought renewed construction activity at Yashodharapura. The focal point of his capital was the temple known as the Phimeanakas. It comprises a single shrine, surrounded by narrow roofed galleries on top of three tiers of laterite, each of descending size. The royal palace would have been built of perishable materials, and will only be traced through excavation of its foundations. These buildings were located within a high laterite wall with five *gopuras*, all ascribed to this reign, enclosing an area 600 × 250 metres in extent. Today, a great plaza lies to the east of this walled precinct. On its eastern side lie the Southern and Northern Khleangs, long sandstone buildings of unknown function. The former belong to the reign of Suryavarman, the latter to Jayaviravarman.

Suryavarman also underlined his authority by beginning the construction of the Western Baray, the largest reservoir at Angkor and one still retaining a considerable body of water. The southern dyke partially covers the temple of Ak Yum, which was still functional in AD 1001. A temple known as the Western Mebon, located on an artificial island in the middle of the reservoir, is in the style of Suryavarman's immediate successor, so although no foundation stelae have been found for the *baray*, it was almost certainly initiated by Suryavarman himself. The energy required in its construction, entailing massive earthen dykes enclosing 17.6 square kilometres, is testament to Suryavarman's organization of labour.

Yet construction activity was not confined to the capital and its environs. In the provinces, the onset of peace allowed several older foundations to be rebuilt. Banteay Srei, Vat Ek and Phnom Chisor were greatly expanded, but no temple of any period matches in magnificence the setting of Preah Vihear. The chosen location on the summit of the Dang Raek range commands an unbroken view to the south across the flat plain of northern Cambodia 550 metres below, which was then dotted with the spires of many foundations. Viewed from below, the golden peaks of Preah Vihear must have seemed the veritable mountain home of the gods. The temple commanding this eyrie was approached by a series of causeways lined by boundary pillars and punctuated by *gopuras*, which contained a corpus of inscriptions. The decoration on these and the principal shrine are rightly renowned for the vigour with which they depict Hindu scenes, such as the popular churning of the ocean of milk. In this ancient Indian epic, Vishnu descends to the bottom of the ocean of milk as the *avatar* Kurma, the turtle, to support Mount Mandara. The mountain is used as a pivot to churn the ocean by demons and gods, to derive *amrita*, the elixir of immortality. Many of the surfaces still bear a red pigment made from haematite, which was probably a base to receive gold leaf.

The inscriptions provide a vibrant glimpse of the purpose of this sacred place and the rituals enacted there. A series of texts on the walls of the second *gopura* hint at royal inspiration for the foundation, because the earliest, dating to AD 1018, describes Suryavarman's establishment of a *linga*, bearing his name as

Suryavarmesvara, here and at other key parts of his realm, including Phnom Chisor to the south. Twenty years later, a further text provides the name of this temple, Sikharesvara, and the name of Sukavarman, the keeper of state archives. He maintained the records of the kings going back to mythical ancestors, which were written on leaves and stored at Preah Vihear and two other named locations.

Preah Vihear was particularly noted for its association with miracles. The texts tell of miraculous events at this temple, and how Sukavarman assiduously maintained a record of all the offerings made as a consequence. The king recognized his loyalty and worth by donating him land, which he renamed Kurukshetra. Finally, the president of the royal court in the *sruk* of Kuti Run ordered Samarendradhipativarman, the inspector of royal service (*rajakarya*) at the temple, to set up an inscription. There are further references to miracles in another text of AD 1038, and to the reincarnation of the god Bhadresvara as Sikharesvara at Preah Vihear, as a result of the king's ascetic devotion. Indeed, the king himself, at Yashodharapura, notified the local dignitaries of the visible manifestation of Sikharesvara, and commanded the populace to maintain the foundation at all times and protect it from its enemies. Clearly, he recognized Preah Vihear as a place of special religious significance.

The countryside after civil war

The mention of enemies at Preah Vihear strikes a chord in other inscriptions across the kingdom. The aftermath of the civil war between Jayaviravarman and Suryavarman saw foundations deserted and destroyed, and, reading between the lines, a scramble for land by those who supported the right side. In AD 1012, for example, Suryavarman gave land to Tapasvindrapandita at Prasat Trapan Run with instructions to manage the foundation and return it to its former prosperity. It was in this climate that so many of the landed aristocratic families raised lengthy inscriptions, which claimed centuries of loyalty and military service to the victorious king. Parakramaviravarman, for example, describes himself in a text from Kuk Prin Crum as the great-grandson of Padma, a minister and a brother-in-law to Jayavarman II, a soldier who was never defeated in battle. He was the chief general of Suryavarman, and marched to war at the head of his army with an irresistible force. He was put in charge of the southern region by the king and destroyed the king's enemy Arjuna. Suryavarman rewarded his general with all the land confiscated from Arjuna. Parakramaviravarman then founded a temple on his new property and donated the merit to the king, thereby ensuring exemptions from tax and the benefit of returns from his new property for himself and his descendants.

Nrpasimhavarman was also a general, fulsomely described as being imbued with heroism, wisdom, power, virtue and glory. He was also the owner of ten villages (*pura*). His brother-in-law was Virendradhipativarman, who had two sons. He was also a general of Suryavarman and a war hero. Nrpasimhavarman solicited land from the king in three places, probably at or near Nak Ta Cih Ko where the inscription was found. The land had either been abandoned or not previously settled, because he cut back the brambles, cleared the forest, founded a village, installed his mother and family, and erected a *linga*. Another faithful retainer and warrior, Lakshmindrapandita, obtained by royal favour gold, gems, and land on which he founded the settlement of Lakshmindrapada. This is described in an inscription dating to 1024–5 from Wat Prah That de Tuk Cha, which begins by telling how the king, who was descended from the maternal line of Indravarman I, severed with his sword the crown of his royal enemy. Lakshmindrapandita had a reservoir and dyke constructed, named Lakshmindratataka after himself, and put in place a golden *linga*. Many endowments were made to the gods, including grain, gold, silver, copper, slaves of both sexes, cattle, land and buffaloes. It is particularly interesting to note the number of reservoirs that he named when delimiting the rice fields, as if their water may have been used for irrigation.

However, like Arjuna above, those who did not support the monarch suffered the consequences. A further text from the vicinity of Yashodharapura describes the property acquired by two men both called Viravarman, an older and a younger, who were presumably related. They bought much land, paying with rice, elephants, gold and ceremonial vessels. But there was retribution from Suryavarman for a man called Hiramya, who was named as his enemy, and whose land was confiscated and given to the younger Viravarman. The king also intervened at Preah Vihear, where the lineage of Pas Khmau, described as being constantly rebellious, had its property confiscated and merged with royal estates.

The social and economic significance of the temple, both as an economic centre and as an instrument of royal influence, is underlined by an inscription from Phnom Sanke Kon, north-west of Angkor. It concerns three brothers and their sister's son. In 1007, they established a *linga* in their ancestral temple, which contained three images of their father Samaraviravarman, each with a different divine name. Nine years later, the king ordered that their temple be linked to that of a larger royal temple, with the requirement that it supply annual tribute. The donation included rice, vegetable oil, sesame seeds, beans, two banners and two garments for the gods.

Under Suryavarman the kingdom expanded from its heartland in the Mekong Valley and round the Great Lake to incorporate the Mun Valley, north of the mountain wall of the Dang Raek range. At Ban Khamoy in Ubon province, we read of a Buddhist foundation, which received various donations including animals, rice, cloth, workers, a pair of buffaloes, four pairs of sacred cattle and a bronze cymbal. This must have been a substantial foundation, for today one can identify one large and two small reservoirs, and the remains of sandstone and laterite structures there. A further Buddhist shrine was located at Phimai, ancient Vimayapura, where an inscription mentions Suryavarman, as well as an offering of rice to the foundation. There is also a concentration of inscriptions relating to land transactions in Battambang province, to the south-west of Angkor, where foundations that suffered from the civil war were restored, and new tracts of land were opened to settlement. Further westward still, a stela from Prachinburi in Thailand describes the king giving land for a religious foundation to Viravardhana, the maternal nephew of Narapatindravarman, brother of Queen Nrpatindralakshmi.

The most revealing of the inscriptions from this part of the kingdom, however, comes from Sdok Kok Thom. This sanctuary today has a central tower of laterite and sandstone, accompanied by two libraries within a court measuring 60 × 40 metres. A high laterite wall encloses a second court reached by a *gopura* to the east, and a moat lies between the two courts. A *baray* 400 × 500 metres in extent lies beyond the enclosures. This site gives an idea of the structure of a provincial establishment often described in the epigraphic record, but its significance lies in its own inscription. Although most commonly referred to for the information it contains on the *devaraja*, a cult established with the consecration of Jayavarman II two centuries previously, the inscription illustrates how, over at least eight generations, a noble family progressively enlarged and improved its estates and wealth. In this context, the disruptions caused by the war of succession that saw Suryavarman accede were potentially catastrophic.

The text covers the family's history from the reign of Jayavarman II until the foundation in AD 1052 at Badraniketana, the old name of the site, of a *linga* called Jayendravarmesvara. Although the inscription was erected under Suryavarman's successor, it describes events during his reign. It not only establishes the land titles held by family members, but also reveals the strenuous steps taken to restore the economic viability of the various properties; to reinstate old and set up new images of ancestors and gods; and to further the standing of the family at court.

The individual responsible for the inscription, Sadasiva, was a courtier of extremely high status who was given successively the exalted titles *kamsten an* Jayendrapandita and *dhuli jen vrah kamraten an* Jayendravarman. The temple incorporated images of his ancestors. A large part of the text concerns land holdings, their clearance, layout and boundaries. We read of offerings and upkeep, of material endowments, slaves, animals and cultural objects. Founders solicited land, which was then divided into *sruk*. Each *sruk* had a temple, which was settled by members of the founder's family. The retainers and workers necessary for the prosperity of the new temple were probably imported, and were grouped into sectors with an indication of their origin. Sadasiva not only solicited the king for land grants and purchased properties, but also continued in the task of restoring the devastated family estates on the death of his predecessor Sivakarya. At Bhadrapattana, he had a reservoir, park and dyke constructed. At Bhadradi, he filled the stable with cattle and dug a dyke. At Vamsahrada, he had a moat, dyke and reservoir built for the prosperity of the estate. The details provided by this inscription open up the possibility of tracing the surviving remains of these various projects.

The achievements of Suryavarman I

The reign of Suryavarman I began in civil war and ended with the restoration of peace and prosperity. In the capital, he initiated the largest reservoir built by any Angkorian king and he founded or re-endowed key regional temples, particularly on the mountain top of Preah Vihear. His loyal followers, bound early in the reign by an oath of loyalty, were rewarded with land grants, and estates ruined by strife were returned to production. Aristocratic families, who traced their ancestry to the very beginning of the kingdom and even beyond, were enabled to restore and embellish their ancestral temples. Suryavarman stands out as being one of the great kings of Angkor.

Udayadityavarman II

Udayadityavarman's relationship with his predecessor is not known. His reign saw a vigorous period of construction at Yashodharapura, and in the provinces there was both

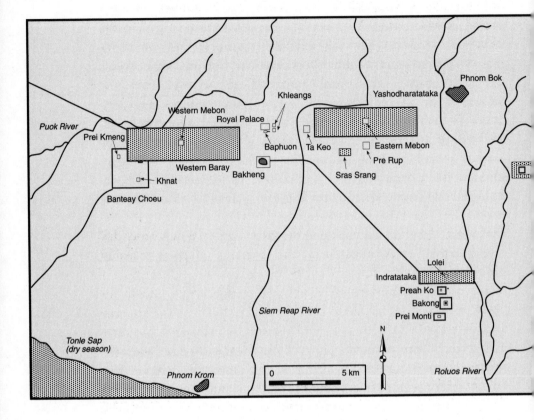

The Western Baray and Baphuon temple mountain were built during the reigns of
Suryavarman I and Udayadityavarman II.

consolidation and spasms of rebellion. The Baphuon, his temple mausoleum, is located just south of the royal precinct, within a stone's throw of the Phimeanakas. An inscription from Lonvek, far to the south-east on the Tonle Sap River, describes how it was built in imitation of Mount Meru, home of the gods. Even today, lacking its central shrine and having suffered several collapses, it is a most impressive monument. The entrance to the second platform is richly decorated with bas-reliefs of exquisite finish, portraying scenes from Hindu epics. We only have written descriptions of the central shrine, said in the Lonvek inscription to have been a tower of gold and by the late thirteenth-century Chinese visitor, Zhou Daguan, to have been a tower of copper.

Zhou Daguan also mentioned the great *barays* that surrounded the capital. The Western Baray, the largest of all, was probably completed in this reign. Recent investigations reveal that it was probably built in stages, each being marked by a north–south dyke as work progressed. Unlike the Eastern Baray, it was excavated below the then ground surface, and the southern dyke is far larger than necessary. It may be that the laterite excavated within the reservoir served as a source of building material. Soft when initially revealed, laterite hardens on exposure to air. It was extensively used in construction, and the core of the Baphuon might well have been built of laterite quarried from such a close and convenient source. There is no doubt that the *baray* was completed at this period, for the Western Mebon in its centre has the architectural style of this reign. This artificial island incorporates a square enclosure demarcated by a wall containing niches and decorative reliefs. Within, there is a water basin with a causeway giving access to a central structure. Part of a huge bronze statue of Vishnu was found here, which recalls a description by Zhou Daguan of a bronze Buddha located on this island sanctuary, out of which water cascaded. He probably mistook Vishnu for the Buddha. The effort expended in the completion of the *baray* and its attendant temple must have involved armies of workers. Its purpose, however, remains a controversial issue, which will be considered below.

The presence of armies of workers, not to mention the members of the court, their families and servants, strongly suggests a dense population. Until this reign, however, we have no information on where people were interred when they died, or the nature of mortuary rituals for the deceased. This situation changed with the chance discovery, at the north-west corner of the Srah Srang reservoir, of a group of three pottery jars containing cremated human remains. They were associated with bronze Buddha images. The French archaeologist B.-P. Groslier then uncovered 1600 square metres of a cemetery, the mortuary jars containing human ashes associated with offerings. There were Chinese ceramic vessels, ceramic figures, bronze mirrors, iron weapons, ingots and pieces of lead. The mortuary jars were grouped with other vessels of local manufacture, a bronze pin 30 centimetres long, iron hooks, chains, axes and knives. A tin vessel was associated with one cremation, along with animal teeth, stone mortars and grinding stones. One pot contained seven lead ingots. In one instance, a pair of bronze mirrors was found, on a precise east–west orientation. The ivory handle survived on another mirror. Bronze images of the Buddha and Vishnu riding the eagle Garuda were also found.

Udayadityavarman's reign was not peaceful, as there were insurrections throughout the kingdom. A certain Kamvau ripped up and destroyed holy images. We learn in a text from Prasat Prah Khset that this rebel general and a host of soldiers initially defeated the loyal army. The great general Sangrama, however, turned defeat into victory and killed him. There was also serious unrest in the south, where Sangrama defeated the rebel leader Aravindhahrada. Narapatindravarman, nephew of a queen of Suryavarman I, restored the settlement of Vrah Damnap, which had been abandoned during these troubles. Royal patronage rewarded loyalty. At Phnom Wan in the upper Mun Valley, a soldier named Viravarman was gifted property and symbols of status, including a golden palanquin and an ivory parasol with peacock plumes. He erected a sanctuary in the settlement of Sukhalaya, endowed it with 200 slaves, land, a herd of buffaloes and other animals. He restored twenty-three villages and built a large reservoir. At Baset, we read of Rajendravarman and Vyapara, two generals, father and son, who served Suryavarman and Udayadityavarman II. The latter king gave Vyapara land when the previous owner died without heirs.

So, despite insurrections and uncertain times, it is clear that loyalty was still rewarded with titles, symbols of status and royal favour; also that the old order of land dealings and the establishment, modification or expansion of family estates continued. Prasat Ta Kham Thom, located in the rich land of the upper Plang River, north-west of Angkor, is a fine example of a provincial establishment, comprising an inner enclosure dominated by a central sanctuary of sandstone reached by four causeways that cross a broad moat. A further moat 100 metres square surrounds this complex, crossed by two *gopuras* to the east and west, and two structures without doors at the north and south. This terrain had been in the family of the author of an inscription since it was gifted to his ancestor by Jayavarman II. First, we read a list of the property he received in exchange for this block of land: silver, clothing, rice, two cattle and a plough. He then describes how he sold his ancestral land in order to provide benefits for his son and grandson.

The inscriptions also reveal other aspects of provincial life. They tell, for example, of an ascetic devotee of Shiva called Jnanapriya Aryamatrin who lived in a religious foundation at Phum Da, which housed a *linga* incorporating the essence of the god. There, in the caves, he and his followers meditated and no doubt enjoyed the water basin, park and flower garden. And further south on the Plain of Reeds, a royal edict decreed that the people of Jitaksetra and other named locations were exempt from all taxes other than on honey and wax, commodities for which the area is still well known.

Harshavarman III, who succeeded his brother in 1066, was also confronted by civil disorder. He enjoyed only a brief reign before further struggles saw the sun set on his dynasty.

CHAPTER 7

THE DYNASTY OF MAHIDHARAPURA: AD 1080–

Jayavarman VI, Dharanindravarman I and the accession of Suryavarman II

In approximately 1080, Jayavarman VI was crowned by the venerable courtier and palace official Divakarapandita, whose remarkable career had seen him, as a young man, participate in the consecration of Udayadityavarman II's golden *linga* at the Baphuon and whose activities provide a common thread through the reigns of the next three Angkorian kings. After receiving sumptuous gifts from the king, including a golden palanquin and parasol, Divakarapandita presided over a major programme of royal merit-making. He offered, on the king's behalf, golden vessels, men and women workers, elephants and horses to all the temples. He also commanded that reservoirs be dug and fine offerings made to all categories of priest, as well as succour given to the poor and homeless. Sacrifices to the gods were ordered and the erection of new images. When the king conducted a pilgrimage to the temples and sacred places, Divakarapandita made the appropriate ritual sacrifices.

Significantly, Jayavarman VI made no attempt to relate his ancestry to previous rulers at Angkor, for this successor to Harshavarman III came not from the plain of Angkor but from the upper Mun Valley across the Dang Raek range in Thailand, a region of broad lowlands rich in salt, laterite and rice fields, and thickly populated during the Iron Age. Jayavarman VI's father,

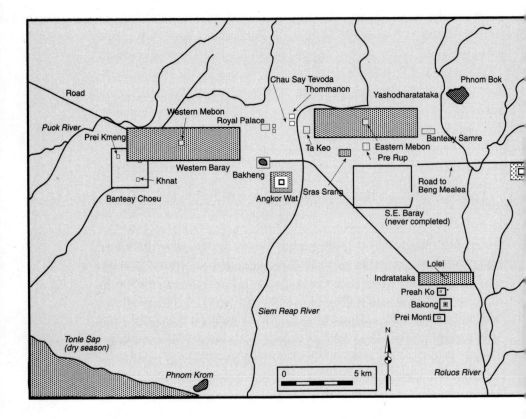

During the reign of Suryavarman II, Angkor Wat was constructed just south of the Bakheng.

who bore royal titles, was presumably a local potentate in this
north-western corner of the kingdom, a border region that had probably enjoyed a loose association with Angkor for some time. His
family is said to have come from Mahidharapura. There is evidence
that Suryavarman had imposed or strengthened his central authority there, and that members of the local dynasty of Mahidharapura
resisted central authority, rose in revolt and seized power
themselves.

In 1875, a certain M. Jules Harmand discovered a splendid stela
in the temple at Ban That, a village on the bank of the Mekong
River in Laos. By the time Étienne Aymonier reached the site
eight years later, it had been damaged by an elephant, but its text
is still legible. It provides a remarkable insight into this noble
family living north of the Dang Raek range, who provided
Jayavarman VI with one of his leading supporters. The description
of Tilaka, a member of this family, reveals the high degree of
learning and status achieved by leading women: 'Of great beauty
and devotion, her divine nature was not disputed.' Her son,
Subhadra, also known as Murdhasiva, immersed himself in the
sacred writings and 'shone like a newly lit fire'. He stood out
among the learned men of his day and, after receiving various
honours from Jayavarman VI, was appointed inspector of sacred
property and religious foundations with the title Bhupendrapan-
dita. Among his responsibilities was the sanctuary of Phnom
Wan.

The area's three major Angkorian centres, Phimai, Phnom Rung
and Phnom Wan, were built on the sites of earlier brick sanctuaries. An inscription dated to AD 921 from Prasat Kravan mentions a
gift of slaves by Sri Mahidharavarman, whose name suggests a
northern base. A later inscription from Phnom Rung sets out
the basis of the genealogy of the new dynasty. It names Hiranyavarman and Hiranyalakshmi as the parents of Jayavarman VI;
his older brother and successor, Dharanindravarman I; and an
unnamed prince. Jayavarman's earliest inscription of 1082, which
comes from Phnom Wan and shows his interest in this foundation, orders Lakshmindravarman, Bhupendravarman and many

other officials including Rajendravarman, general of the royal army of the centre, to care for it.

Jayavarman VI died *circa* 1108 and, as a later inscription from Preah Vihear relates, Divakarapandita was again in attendance at the accession of the dead king's older brother, Dharanindravarman I. Having again conducted the consecration, he arranged for numerous merit-making offerings to be made to the state temples, made sacrificial offerings, erected images, had water basins excavated, and distributed alms to the poor and needy.

Dharanindravarman's reign was short – only six years – and this king, who never sought the throne, has left no known monuments. Yet, as the king's inscriptions testify, the tradition continued of elite families being granted favours by the monarch and augmenting their power and status. These texts are found from Phimai in the north to Phnom Bayang in the south including, interestingly, a short text on a Buddha image from Lopburi in central Thailand, and collectively they indicate the extent of the kingdom. A brief inscription from the sanctuary of Phimai mentions Sri Virendradhipativarman, of the country of Chok Vakula, a general later to appear on the reliefs of Angkor Wat. The king himself ordered the erection of the statue to a divinity in the sanctuary of Bhadresvarasrama at Phnom Bayang, west of the Bassac River. It was endowed with workers assigned for each half of the month, and rice for officiants.

Two of the most revealing inscriptions concern the landholdings and foundations of two families related to the royal family. The first comes from the village of Samrong, a bare 5 kilometres north-east of Angkor, and dates to AD 1093–4. It was erected by Yogisvarapandita, a nephew by marriage of a daughter of Suryavarman I, and the principal purpose of the text is to list a series of transactions in which land was purchased by Yogisvarapandita and donated to religious foundations. He must have been extremely wealthy, for the list of properties is long, and he was at pains to reveal that the endowments were to be overseen by the head of the foundation, not by any member of his family. The purchase was made with cattle, silver, bronze and tin

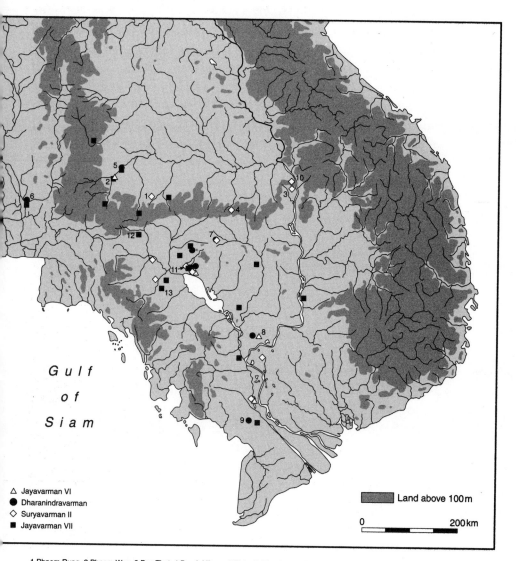

Jayavarman VI
Dharanindravarman
Suryavarman II
Jayavarman VII

Land above 100 m

Gulf

of

Siam

0   200 km

1 Phnom Rung, 2 Phnom Wan, 3 Ban That, 4 Preah Vihear, 5 Phimai, 6 Lopburi, 7 Phnom Sandak, 8 Yay Hom, 9 Phnom Bayang,
10 Wat Phu, 11 Wat Kok Po, 12 Banteay Chmar, 13 Baset

The distribution of inscriptions for the dynasty of Mahidharapura.

III

vessels, gold rings, cloth, elephants, vehicles, salt, rice and goats. He further gifted workers, and took steps to build a reservoir and gardens supplied with pure water. The administrative details include the provision of workers and land to sustain the foundation for each half of the month.

Another member of the royal family, Nrpendradhipativarman – brother-in-law of Jayavarman VI and Dharanindravarman I, and a chief of the army – received a number of royal land grants. He also recorded the endowment of a hermitage called Nrpendrasrama, together with a gold image of the sacred bull Nandi in an inscription, of which he was the author, at Phnom Sandak, a low hill about 75 kilometres north-east of Angkor. A sanctuary formerly known as Shivapura lies on the top, which comprises a court on the east, opening via a *gopura* into a walled enclosure measuring 60 × 40 metres. Five large and three smaller towers, together with two galleries, lie within. The inscriptions found here date from the reigns of Yashovarman I to Suryavarman II, so the foundation has a long history.

Further insight into another family with royal affiliations comes from Yay Hom, situated in the low-lying terrain east of the Tonle Sap River. It is a double-walled sanctuary measuring 300 × 200 metres containing a sandstone temple that in turn is linked to a large *baray*. The author of the Sanskrit text, Hiranyalakshmi, was the great-niece of Jayavarman VI and describes her ascetic devotion to Buddhism, an interesting portent of the rise of this religion in the later history of this dynasty.

Suryavarman II

Dharanindravarman I's reign ended violently. When still a young man, his great-nephew, Suryavarman II, had already removed a rival claimant about whom we know nothing except his likely descent from the line of Harshavarman III. Then he turned on his great-uncle, Dharanindravarman. The Ban That inscription described his entering into a terrible battle with the royal army during which he leapt onto the king's elephant and killed him, just as the eagle Garuda takes a snake in its talons. He then set about unifying a kingdom which had fragmented under the benign rule of his predecessor. Vassal kings paid him tribute. He built three stone towers like the summits of Mount Meru with enclosing walls, a series of shrines and great *barays*, surrounded by groves of flowering plants that were populated by celestial beings and holy men. With its banners floating in the breeze, the harmonious music reaching up to the sky, the sound of singing and the sight of the dancers, this place was designed to resemble the paradise of Indra.

In AD 1113, the venerable Divakarapandita anointed Suryavarman II and, in a compelling image of the importance of ritual and merit making in an inscription from Preah Vihear, we read of the king studying sacred rituals, celebrating all the religious festivals and making gifts to Divakarapandita, who performed sacrifices to the spirits of the ancestors. These gifts included two fans of peacock feathers with golden handles, four white parasols, ear ornaments and rings, bracelets, pectorals and golden bowls, workers, elephants and sacred brown-coloured cattle.

The august priest then embarked on a pilgrimage to make offerings at holy shrines, beginning at Wat Phu on the bank of the Mekong River. The king had provided him with a script to be engraved on all goods donated to temples. Divakarapandita gifted valuables, had water basins dug and named after himself, endowed villages and workers, and founded hermitages. We can gain insight into the extent of his merit making through his list of daily offerings to this foundation: rice, oil, sacred cloth, tapers, incense, dancers, singers, musicians and flower vases. This was not all. At Preah Vihear, he provided a golden statue of dancing Shiva. The villages that he donated were all supplied with water basins and the requirements for daily rituals. He covered the floor of the towers with a facing of bronze, and gifted standards, tiered parasols and fine fabric to swathe the towers, the courts and the avenue leading to the site where the ritual of burning the rice took place. He gave gifts annually to the priests, religious officiants, the provincial governor and all the serving people. Identical largesse was dispensed at the shrine of Phnom Sandak and Wat Kok Po.

He then turned his attention to the temple of Banteay Srei (the citadel of women), which had been given him by the king. He restored the foundation to the worship of Shiva, as was its original intention. Finally, we can appreciate the central control of labour when we read that the king ordered royal artisans of the first, second, third and fourth categories, and the people of the district of Sadya, to construct for Divakarapandita and his descendants a tower, a *baray* and a surrounding wall.

Phnom Rung, north of the Dang Raek range, is one of the finest provincial temple complexes from the Angkorian period. The long entrance avenue and fine proportions of the central precinct enhance its hilltop setting. Looking to the south from the sanctuary, one can see the nearby temple of Muang Tam and its associated *baray*, while beyond lies the ridge of the Dang Raek chain. Here we find an inscription that gives the ancestry of Suryavarman. There was, it says, a king called Hiranyavarman, the father of Jayavarman VI and Dharanindravarman I. King Ksitindraditya, a grandson of Hiranyavarman, was the father of Suryavarman. Narendraditya, a cousin of the king, was responsible for the monument of Phnom Rung. His son Hiranya erected a gold image to him there.

Suryavarman was one of the great kings of the civilization of Angkor and his patronage, already described, gives some insight into the role of ritual and merit making. Angkor Wat, his enduring temple mausoleum, is often described as the largest and finest religious monument ever completed. His achievement is the greater because other superb buildings also date to this reign. In addition, he reopened diplomatic relations with China, but the darker side to his rule was a series of unsuccessful, even disastrous, military campaigns against the kingdom's traditional enemies east of the Truong Son range: the Chams. In surveying his reign, we are for the first time able to see images of an Angkorian king and his court on the bas-reliefs of Angkor Wat.

This monument is without question the outstanding achievement of the civilization of Angkor. Curiously, there are no direct references to it in the epigraphic record, so we do not know its original name and controversy remains over its function and aspects of its symbolic status. Early Portuguese visitors refer to a large inscription, which was probably the foundation stela, but it has since been lost. We do, however, know that the temple was dedicated to Vishnu and it opens to the west, that god's quarter of the compass. Angkor Wat today is but a pale reflection of its former state. Traces of gilded stucco survive on the central tower, and a Japanese visitor in the early seventeenth century noted gilding over the stone bas-reliefs. It must in its heyday have literally been a golden temple. A 4-metre-high statue of Vishnu, which might once have been located in the central sanctuary tower, is still to be seen in the western entrance building. It remains venerated to this day.

The first indication of the magnitude of Angkor Wat is the scale of the surrounding moat. It is 200 metres wide, and is retained on both inner and outer banks by laterite and sandstone walls, which cover a distance of about 10 kilometres. Each huge block of sandstone is individually cut to fit perfectly against the next. The inner edge of the moat gives way to a flat expanse beyond which lies an enclosing wall 4.5 metres high. There are four entrances, the largest being on the western side, where the *gopura* is equipped with five portals. The central doorway links the bridge across the moat with the temple via a causeway flanked by balustrades in the form of *nagas*. On either side lie two small temples and two rectangular water basins. The causeway leads to a cruciform platform and then to the three galleries and central tower, which comprise the heart of the complex.

The bas-reliefs that cover the walls of the third, outermost gallery illustrate for the first time a king and his court. Even after the vicissitudes of eight centuries, they are an astonishing tour de force, but in their heyday, when some if not all of the figures were covered in gold, they must have been even more impressive. For the social historian, the depictions of a royal audience and a court progress are the most valuable. Suryavarman, larger than life, is seen seated on a wooden throne. He wears an elaborate crown and pectoral, heavy ear ornaments, armlets, bracelets and anklets. He holds what looks like a dead snake in his right hand and an unidentified object in his left. A forest of fourteen parasols, five large fans and four fly whisks surround him as he receives his ministers. Inscriptions name them. Virasimhavarman offers him a scroll. Vardhana and Dhananjaya hold a hand over their hearts to indicate loyalty and deference. A fourth is described as the inspector of merits and defects.

The audience is followed by a progression down the mountainside. The king rides an elephant, and is accompanied by the *raja-hotar*, or royal priest. The great generals in this military parade ride on their elephants. There is Virendradhipativarman, who in 1108 had the image of Trailokyavijaya erected in the sanctuary of Phimai. He is surrounded by nine parasols. Ahead of him in the column comes Jayayuddhavarman with eight parasols. His troops wear distinctive helmets with deer-head images. Rajasinghavarman has thirteen parasols and two banners, but pride of place, naturally, goes to *vrah pada kamraten an paramavishnuloka* (the sacred feet of the lord who has gone to live with Vishnu), the king. He has fifteen parasols, five fans, six fly whisks, four banners and, in front of his elephant, a standard of Vishnu riding Garuda. Even his elephant wears a splendid jewelled headdress. The king's presence is signalled by the sacred fire being carried aloft, and an orchestra of trumpets, conches, drums and a gong. We also obtain a glimpse of the women of the court, princesses borne in fine palanquins as they travel through a forest, one adjusting her hair, another checking her appearance. We also see serried ranks of foot soldiers and cavalry, stolid rows of Khmer and loosely drilled, long-haired troops labelled Syem, which might indicate either that they came from Siam or, alternatively, that they were dark-skinned vassals.

Many Angkorian inscriptions conclude with lines threatening punishment for those who injure the foundation and rewards for the faithful supporters. At Angkor Wat, the fate of the former and the heavenly abode of the latter are graphically portrayed. Again, small inscriptions in the walls describe the punishments for particular crimes, the fate of each person being determined by Yama, god of death, who sits in judgement on a water buffalo. These crimes include theft of land, houses, animals, rice, liquor, shoes and parasols. Incendiaries are also destined for severe punishment, as are those guilty of gluttony and greed. Punishments were indeed draconian. The guilty were crushed under heavy rollers, or suspended upside down from trees and beaten. On the other hand, those with a spotless life on earth were rewarded with a delightful existence in celestial palaces.

Scenes from Hindu epics fill other sections of the gallery walls. The most impressive is undoubtedly the depiction of the churning of the ocean of milk in search of the elixir of immortality, but the battles of Lanka and Kurukshetra also bring home the nature of warfare at this period, dominated, it seems, by vicious hand-to-hand slaughter.

A circuit of the bas-reliefs ends where it began, and progress towards the central tower is via a large columned building, which contains four sunken water basins and, formerly, statues of gods. Steps then lead up to a second gallery and beyond to the heart of the monument with its central tower rising up in the form of a lotus. It was here, in 1935, that French archaeologist Georges Trouvé excavated the 27-metre-deep shaft, then filled with water, to recover the sacred deposit of two white sapphires and two gold leaves.

The demand for labour to construct a monument on this scale must have exceeded all previous experience. Not only is the weight of stone extraordinary, but virtually every surface bears decorative carving of the highest quality, none more so than the *apsaras*, heavenly maidens, which astonish and delight.

There have been many attempts to understand the purpose and symbolic meaning of this monument. Most agree that the five central towers represent the peaks of Mount Meru, the home of the gods, while the moat symbolizes the surrounding ocean. Eleanor Mannika has sought deeper symbolic structures through the medium of the monument's dimensions and its relationship to the annual movements of the sun and moon, but this initiative has invoked some scepticism. There is also debate about the ultimate purpose of Angkor Wat. Did the outer wall enclose residential areas and the king's palace, as has been suggested by Claude Jacques? Was it designed for the worship of Vishnu, or was it also built as a temple and mausoleum for Suryavarman? There is no specific allusion to his mortuary rites, but it is probable that Angkor Wat was not completed in his lifetime, for the depiction of him at court and in a progress is accompanied by his posthumous name, Paramavishnuloka, 'he who has entered the heavenly world of Vishnu'.

Georges Cœdès, however, is specific on the purpose of Angkor Wat. It was at first a monument to the king, portrayed as divine, where he had communion with the gods. At death, the king's remains were placed in the central tower of Angkor to animate his image. A stone container has been recovered from this tower, 1.4 metres long, 80 centimetres wide and 72 centimetres high. It resembles an example from Banteay Samre, which retained the original lid. No such container from any Angkorian site has been found in its original position or with its contents intact, but their location, and the fact that each has a hole in the base, suggest a funerary function. The hole, for example, would have enabled liquid of putrefaction to seep out of the container. South-East Asian royal mortuary rituals retain the custom of placing the body in such a container prior to cremation. In Bali, for example, the king was cremated, then part of the ashes were placed in a stone container and interred under a stone temple. Worship of the dead king ensued once his soul entered his stone image, thus permitting contact with the ancestors of the dynasty. Within this mortuary tradition, Angkor Wat should be seen as the preserve of the immortal sovereign merged with Vishnu, in a heaven populated by the celestial *apsaras*.

The construction of Angkor Wat did not stop further building activity beyond the capital. Work also commenced at Beng Mealea (meaning lotus pool), a vast complex 40 kilometres east of the capital. This enigmatic sanctuary has yielded no inscriptions nor extensive bas-reliefs, but stylistically and in terms of the scenes from Hindu epics, it belongs to the period of Angkor Wat. It is associated with a large *baray* with a temple in its centre, while a canal links the site with the Great Lake. Jacques has suggested that this might have been a means of transporting the local sandstone to Angkor. Chau Say Tevoda and the Thommanon, which lie close to each other between the Yashodharatataka and the Phimeanakas, are small shrines built during this period. Banteay Samre, 10 kilometres to the north-east of Angkor Wat, is a substantial sanctuary with two enclosures and a large basin to the east. It is likely that Preah Khan of Kompong Svay, Preah Vihear and Wat Phu were also added to during this reign.

Although Angkor Wat and the construction of or additions to other great temples dominate our attention, there was much activity in the provinces. The king continued to reward faithful retainers with land grants such as that to Vagindrapandita at Wat Sla Ku, adjacent to the Tonle Sap River. It consisted of vacant and weed-infested land that could now be brought into cultivation. The new owner cleared the property, uprooted large trees and provided a home for ascetics. Houses were built, a reservoir dug for the benefit of the community, while boundary markers demarcated rice fields.

Trapan Don On lies just north-west of Angkor, and its important inscription recounts the successful career of Namasivaya, a royal servant who, like Divakarapandita, became increasingly important and wealthy over the course of a long career covering the reigns of four kings. He entered the service of Udayadityavarman II as a herdsman with responsibility for the sacred cattle at the age of eighteen. He then served under Harshavarman III and Jayavarman VI, who elevated him to head of the royal herdsmen, in which role he led the cattle in a procession round the royal palace. As he continued in this position under Dharanindravarman I and Suryavarman II, so he was rewarded with land by royal favour and grew to be sufficiently wealthy to institute meritorious acts. He bought further land; invested in a reservoir and moat, bridges, fences and walls; and finally offered all the merit of his pious works to his king. Yet the text not only describes what Namasivaya achieved, but also gives us valuable information on how the land was allocated and worked. He specifies four categories of land: that for the maintenance of the temple, for the temple officiants, for the chief functionary and, lastly, the common land for the agricultural labourers. Nineteen such workers are listed, ten men and nine women, although there were probably more, and they were divided into two groups. The first group worked the temple fields for the fifteen light days of the month, the other for the dark periods of a waning moon. When released from the two-weekly commitment to supply the temple, the labourers would have been free to till land for their own maintenance.

According to Chinese records, Suryavarman sent embassies to China and increased the conflict with his Cham neighbours. The hostile relations that ensued had severe repercussions. The period between the death of Suryavarman II in 1150 and the accession of Jayavarman VII in 1181 was evidently one of internal strife, which exposed the Khmer to a catastrophic defeat at the hands of the Chams.

Retrospective inscriptions describe how Suryavarman was succeeded by a cousin, Dharanindravarman II. The latter reigned for no more than a decade, and was probably succeeded by a relative under the name of Yashovarman II. There was then a struggle for power involving an upstart of no identified royal ancestry known as Tribhuvanadityavarman (meaning protégé of the sun of three worlds). Having killed Yashovarman II, he had to face an attack from Champa led by their king Jaya Indravarman in 1177. As far as the sources disclose, this involved a water-borne invasion, up the Mekong and Tonle Sap rivers, and then across the Tonle Sap itself. Angkor was sacked and King Tribhuvanadityavarman killed. According to the great inscription of the Phimeanakas, the future king was then in Champa, and, hearing of the attack, hurried back to Cambodia. Emerging from the wings to centre stage, he defeated the Chams in battles that probably took place on the Great Lake and in Angkor itself, and was crowned in 1181.

Jayavarman VII and the Bayon

The reign of Jayavarman VII was both a high water mark and a turning of the tide of Angkorian history. The present layout of Angkor is the result of his intensive building programme. The city known today as Angkor Thom was his creation. A foundation stela from one of the corner temples metaphorically describes the king as the groom and the city as his bride. The new city encloses earlier foundations, including the Baphuon and the Phimeanakas. It has, as its outer limits, a moat crossed by four bridges placed in the centre of each side and one extra entrance on the eastern wall. The walls located beyond the moat are about 3 kilometres long on each side, and are pierced by 23-metre-high entrance gateways, which lie at the end of two rows of gods and demons holding a *naga*. The entrance gateways were dominated by colossal heads in sandstone, each looking towards one of the cardinal points of the compass.

The Bayon temple, described by Jayavarman's wife as Madhyadri, lies in the centre of the city and reveals the incorporation of large heads on the temple towers. These have been seen as representations of the king as a *bodhisattva*, an enlightened one. This vast and complex structure went through at least three phases of expansion and modification. The outer enclosing wall contains eight cruciform entrance towers, and is covered in bas-reliefs that depict battle scenes and the daily activities of ordinary people. On the third level, one is confronted by the multitude of towers and profusion of enormous heads gazing serenely into the distance. The central shrine, unusually, is circular and must originally have been gilded. A deep shaft under this tower contained the broken parts of a large image of the Buddha, a find reflecting the reaction against Buddhism after the king's death.

The outer walls of the Bayon are decorated with a series of bas-reliefs that provide an unparalleled glimpse of life during the reign

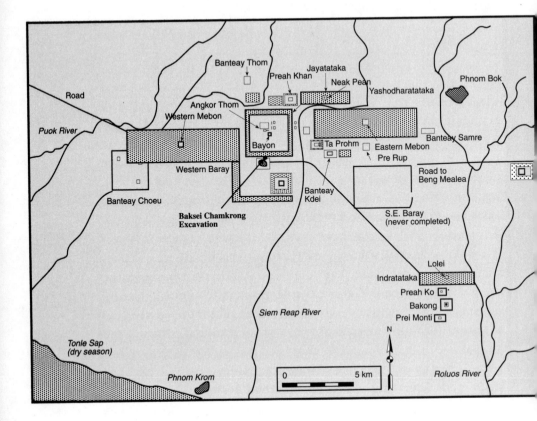

Angkor during the reign of Jayavarman VII saw many new monuments, and an entirely new city of Angkor Thom. The two major new temples were Preah Khan and Ta Prohm.

of Jayavarman VII. The scenes include battles on land and water, feasting, life in a rich person's house, hunting, playing games, selling in the market, cooking and even fashioning and raising the wood to build a palace.

Depictions of Jayavarman's victories dominate many of the reliefs. We can see an army on the march, the generals aloft on their elephants, the infantry below, one group holding battle standards. Some soldiers push a wheeled vehicle on which they have mounted a ballista for firing a large projectile. Similar weapons, not seen on the reliefs from Angkor, are borne by elephants. The Khmer foot soldiers wear their hair short or tied at the back. Their ear lobes are distended by the insertion of an ornament, and they carry a round shield in one hand and a spear in the other. One group carries what looks like a large and heavy gong or drum. The Chams, on the other hand, carry curiously shaped crescentic shields and have elaborate headdresses. Their warships are highly decorated and are propelled by oarsmen.

One of the most informative scenes, in terms of revealing the contrasting lives of aristocrats and their servants, shows a feast in a forest. In the lower register, we see the cooks preparing food. Some grill fish, while a man pours rice into a cooking vessel. Others fill dishes to be taken to the feast on trays that are borne on the waiters' heads. A pig is about to be placed in a cauldron while a cook below fans the flames. In the second register above, the nobles are being served food and they are seen conversing and eating while seated on the ground. The surrounding trees teem with birds and monkeys.

A second feasting scene takes us into the house of a rich Chinese merchant. Again, we see domestic staff preparing food in cooking vessels of various sizes, which stand over what looks like a modern style of charcoal stove. Above, the master and his guests sit on raised seats, holding cups. Servants are offering food. This relief illuminates the lifestyle of a rich person. We can see the columns, the ornamented roof and the ridge tiles, while wine containers and parasols hang from the ceiling.

Almost incidentally, we can explore the world of Angkor and find out more about everyday activities. In one scene, a woman in a pavilion is being helped in labour. In another, two men are intent on a game of chess. We can almost hear the sound of the chisel in the scene that shows men shaping building stones and lifting them with the aid of a lever. We can see men casting their nets and hauling in fish, and women selling the daily catch in a market. A man carries baskets that might contain rice; another drives an ox cart indistinguishable from its modern counterpart. A crowd of onlookers watches a cockfight and in another scene, two boars are spoiling for a fight. Finally, we are taken to the Great Lake, to witness the arrival of a Chinese trading junk. It is refreshing indeed to be provided, as it were, with a newsreel of everyday scenes after the solid diet of endowments and land boundaries that dominate the inscriptions.

The Jayatataka, Ta Prohm, Preah Khan and Banteay Chmar

The royal palace lay north of the Bayon, where today one finds a walled precinct dominated by the temple of the Phimeanakas. Tranquil basins lie between this temple and the northern enclosing wall. To the east, this precinct opens to the terrace of the elephants, a 300-metre-long raised platform, which may once have supported gilded pavilions. It comprises a front wall decorated with elephants close to life size, and gives the impression of being a reviewing stand for the court to witness processions or major events. A second raised area, the so-called terrace of the leper king, lies to the north. This takes its name from a statue of Yama, god of death, which is thought to indicate signs of leprosy. Cœdès has suggested that this area was set aside for royal cremations, but the evidence is fugitive. The facing wall bears scenes based on Hindu myths and conceals a second, earlier wall with similar scenes.

To the east of the new city, the king ordered the construction of a reservoir, known as the Jayatataka, 3.7 × 9 kilometres in extent. The island in the middle housed Rajasri (Neak Pean), one of the most exquisite of all Angkorian temples. The tower in the centre is ringed by two *nagas* with tails entwined, and water from the surrounding pond flows through four figures into their own basin. In one chapel, water spurted through the mouth of an elephant; in the others there were figures of a horse, a lion and a human. The contemporary inscriptions tell us that the complex is a replica of Lake Anavatapta, a sacred Himalayan lake imbued with miraculous curative powers to remove human sins. There must have been a regular passage of pilgrims across the water of the Jayatataka to visit this holy shrine.

The old *baray* of Srah Srang was also slightly reduced in area during this reign, and enclosed by stone steps. Excavations in the north-west corner have uncovered a working place, littered with large pieces of stone, gutter stones, stone chips, axes, adzes, knives, whetstones and polishers. This workshop could have been associated with the new works on the Srah Srang, or the adjacent temple of Banteay Kdei.

Jayavarman founded two enormous temple complexes beyond the walls of Angkor Thom, Rajavihara (Ta Prohm) and Nagara Jayasri (Preah Khan), to honour, respectively, his mother and his father. The former has been left untouched, and gives the visitor a clear impression of how other temples must have appeared before the clearance of vegetation and reconstruction. Within a wall of laterite a kilometre long and 600 metres wide lie two courts enclosed by passageways, each containing many small single-chambered temples.

The foundation stela of this great temple was written by Sri Suryakumara (meaning the sun prince), one of the king's sons, and was set in place in 1186. Jayavarman's maternal ancestry was stressed, while his father's line is barely mentioned, save that he descended from those who lived at Mahidharapura. One reason for this is that the king's mother, Srijayarajacudamani, came from the old royal lineage, which in the text of the inscription goes back even as far as mythical ancestors including Srutavarman and Sresthavarman.

After his victory over the Chams and his consecration as king, Jayavarman showered gifts, titles and property on his *guru*, including a golden palanquin with ribbons, banners with peacock plumes, parasols and fans with golden handles and the title Sri Jayamangalarthadeva. The temple also housed many statues of divinities. Étienne Aymonier, who found the inscription in 1885, also recovered three statues, one of which the local people called Ta Prohm, or ancestor Brahma, a name now applied to the temple. The principal image, covered, it is said, in gems, represented the king's mother in the form of the mother of Buddha. There were also many other images. Indrakumara mentions 260 that occupied the shrines. Brief inscriptions name the statues that once stood within. Some reveal the names of a founder's parents incorporating the title -isvara, indicating incorporation of the qualities of the Bodhisattva Lokesvara. Thus, the parents of Nrpendrapandita are named as Nrpendresvara representing the father, and Nrpendresvari the mother. This suggests that the complex incorporated not only the principal image of the king's mother, but also family shrines containing images of the ancestors of members of his court. Appreciating this reveals the monument as a centre for the worship of deified ancestors.

The visitor today can ramble over ruins, still encumbered by the invasive forest, where trees envelop the temples and roots split apart the walls. But the inscription provides a glimpse of the temple in its heyday, showing how such an institution was a symbol of both royal and dynastic power and a generator of both religious and economic activity, around which a whole society in miniature operated. It also reveals some unexpected aspects of life in Jayavarman VII's kingdom, which do not seem out of place today. Eighteen high priests and 2740 officials lived and worked there, together with 2202 assistants, which included 615 female dancers. In total, 12,640 people had the right to lodge within. Feeding and clothing this multitude involved the provision of rice, honey, molasses, oil, fruit, sesame, millet, beans, butter, milk, salt and vegetables, all the quantities being scrupulously listed for appropriation from the royal foundations and warehouses. Clothing was also required, and even the number of mosquito nets is set down. Assigned to supply the temple were 66,265 men and women, a figure rising to 79,365 if you include Burmese and Chams. The inscription then provides an inventory of the foundation's assets: gold and silver vessels; 35 diamonds; 40,620 pearls; 4540 precious stones such as beryl; copper goblets; tin; lead; 512 silk beds; 876 veils from China; cushions; and 523 sunshades. There were musical instruments 'to charm the spirit' and, with nightfall or for rituals, there were 165,744 wax torches.

There was also a highly organized healthcare system. The foundation was responsible for the administration of 102 hospitals strategically placed across the kingdom, some of which have been identified on the basis of their own inscriptions. The foundation stelae are all identical, as is their basic design, which includes a chapel housing an image of Buddha the healer and an exterior pond. These absorbed considerable quantities of food and other supplies, and the list provides us with a veritable Angkorian pharmacopoeia. There were 81,640 men and women from 838 villages assigned to supply these hospitals with rice, clothing, honey, wax and fruit. The doctors were supplied with two varieties of camphor, coriander, pepper, mustard, cardamoms, molasses, cumin, pine resin, ginger, onions and ointment made from ten plants for the treatment of fevers. Also on hand were 1960 boxes of salve to ease haemorrhoids. The staff of each institution comprised two doctors and their assistants, two dispensary workers, two cooks who also assisted in cleaning, water heaters, specialists in preparing medicines and various other attendants, not least the temple servants who prepared the offerings to the Buddha.

The final stanzas in this foundation document bring us to the king's intention: the principal image took the form of his mother as Prajnaparamita, perfection of wisdom, and parent of the Buddha. The temple was founded to make merit for her salvation. He exhorted all future kings to honour this intention and safeguard it against thieves and sacrilege.

Nagara Jayasri, the holy city of victory, is a second temple complex built by royal order. Known today as Preah Khan, it lies just outside the north-eastern corner of Angkor Thom and on the same orientation as the Jayatataka. Indeed, there is a landing stage that links the *baray* with the eastern entrance to the temple. The traditional construction of a temple mountain comprising a series of platforms was no longer followed. The buildings of Preah Khan are on the same level, surrounded by a moat and wall 800 metres × 700 metres in extent. Access is by four causeways flanked by gods and giants who hold *naga* snakes. The interior incorporates two enclosures with numerous shrines and intervening courts. Brief inscriptions associated with the shrines detail the names of the images within and their instigator. Again, there are examples of an individual setting in place images of his ancestors.

The foundation stela was written by Virakumara, another of Jayavarman's sons, who stated that it was built on the very site where his father had defeated the Chams. Its ultimate purpose was to make merit for the king's father, whose image under the likeness of Bodhisattva Lokesvara was consecrated in 1191. This statue was located in the central shrine, and was accompanied by 283 other images. The foundation inscription then follows the same course as that from Ta Prohm. There is a eulogy to the king and a description of his ancestry. The number and placement of images to a pantheon of gods is then set out. There was one in the rice warehouse, four in the pilgrims' rest house and three in the hospital. Twenty-four were placed in the four entrances to the temple. Beyond the confines of Preah Khan, fourteen were erected on the island that housed the temple of Rajyasri (Neak Pean) in the centre of the Jayatataka. There were more in the shrines flanking this reservoir, making a total of 515.

The text then enumerates the food needed to sustain the gods, listing rice, sesame, peas, butter, fresh milk, honey and molasses. There follows a list of 645 lengths of white and red cloth to clothe the gods, as well as for bedding and seating. Silk mosquito nets were required to protect the deities. Food for the temple officials, with special reference to the New Year and feast days, is then set out in a list that includes oil, used possibly as a cosmetic after ritual ablutions. The grand total of offerings includes pine resin, presumably for lighting and tapers, 423 goats and 360 pigeons as well as peacocks. The king, together with the owners, assigned no fewer than 5324 villages housing 97,840 people to the service of this temple, including cooks and 1000 dancers. As with Ta Prohm, the inscription proceeds with an inventory of temple property, which includes, apart from large quantities of gold and silver vessels, precious stones, 112,300 pearls and a brown cow with gilded horns and hoofs.

The inscription then lists twenty-three locations favoured with a statue of Jayabuddhamahanatha, which, as Cœdès has suggested, probably represented the king as Buddha. Identifying every site is not possible, but some can be traced with confidence. Thus Lavodayapura is Lopburi, Svarnapura is Suphanburi, Jayarajapuri is Ratburi, and Jayasimhapuri is probably Muang Singh. The last site is located in the far west of Thailand, and comprises a walled city with a central shrine constructed of laterite and covered in stucco. This area was strategically important for the control of trade over the Three Pagodas Pass linking central Thailand with Burma, but unfortunately no inscriptions have been found there to clarify its foundation and governance. It may have been a further example of the imposition of central control over a remote province during a period of relative strength. Wat Mahathat at Lopburi is another foundation that probably reflects Angkorian political dominance of some form in central Thailand.

In a further listing of his father's achievements, Virakumara describes the construction of 121 rest houses for travellers, many of whom were probably making pilgrimages to holy shrines such as the Rajyasri. Fifty-seven were placed on the road to the capital of Champa, and seventeen on the road to the king's ancestral home at Phimai. There must have been a wide choice of destinations, for the inscription lists 20,400 statues of gods in gold, silver, bronze and stone across the kingdom, requiring appropriation of goods and services from 208,532 men and women from 8176 villages. This number included 923 supervisors, 6465 workmen and 1622 female dancers, but the majority must have laboured hard to produce the huge quantities of rice and cloth listed.

The annual round of devotions in the temple is illustrated by a listing of the deities, probably small reproductions of the actual statues that were assembled at Preah Khan for special rituals. The list includes Jayarajacudamani, the deified mother of the king, from Preah Khan; the Jayabuddhamahanatha images outlined above; the god Campesvara from Phimai, and others to a total of 122. Again, we find a list of requirements for this service, to be obtained from the royal warehouses: gold, silver, tin, rice, honey, beeswax, milk, pine resin, 459 items of clothing for the gods and 143 boxes of perfume.

The king, so the inscription then says, built the Jayatataka, the great *baray* that abuts Preah Khan to the east. From the landing stage there, one could embark for the island with the temple of Rajyasri (Neak Pean), where contact with the water would wash away the slime of sins and serve as 'a vessel to travel the ocean of existences'. Looking at the same view today, all that one sees are rice fields and perhaps a herd of cattle advancing towards the temple entrance. One needs the original words of the prince to appreciate the heavenly scene of the gilded temple giving access to the sacred lake with its holy island that offered redemption from sins.

The merit that accrued with the endowment of this great foundation was especially dedicated to the king's father, to whom he was devoted. Many others also made merit with donations to these temples. The great stela of the Phimeanakas comprises a eulogy of Queen Jayarajadevi, sister of the author of the inscription, Indradevi. It mentions both Ta Prohm and Preah Khan, to which Jayarajadevi had offered ritual objects and where she had placed her riches at the disposal of the gods and the poor. To Jayarajacudamani, she gave two gold statues of Nandi (the sacred ox), four gold eagles and an eternally burning lamp. To Jayasri (Neak Pean), she donated a pair of gold images of Nandin, lions, a mirror, a magnificent fly whisk of gold, a golden stool of 'inconceivable beauty', a golden box, a crown of gold and two villages. To the god of Madhyadri (the Bayon), she donated 100 banners of Chinese fabric, and she re-covered with gold the temple Vasudhatilaka (probably the Phimeanakas), which had been despoiled and looted by the Chams. More distant shrines also benefited. The god Campesvara at Phimai received a drum of gilded silver. To the temple of Jayaksetrasiva (Baset, near Battambang), she gave an image of the god Jayarajamahesvara. More practically, the queen made merit by providing a foundation for a hundred girls abandoned by their mothers.

Jayavarman's major temple foundations were not confined to Angkor. In a remote part of north-western Cambodia, Jayavarman founded and endowed Banteay Chmar. Aymonier was fortunate enough to visit this site before time and looters had taken their toll, and he placed it only behind Angkor Wat and the Bayon in terms of size and wealth of decoration, not least because of its extensive bas-reliefs. The layout follows precedent. There is a moat and an outer walled enclosure 2.2 kilometres × 2.4 kilometres in extent, which, on the eastern side, is punctured by a reservoir 1.7 kilometres long and 1 kilometre wide. A stream fed this *baray* at its north-east corner, and water flowed into the moat at the south-west corner, where Aymonier noted the paved outlet that controlled the water level. The overflow then filled the moat that runs around the outer walls. The temple in the middle of the reservoir incorporates an oval bank within which lie four basins, two of which are curved and two of which are circular. A further oval bank lies inside these basins, with the temple at the centre. The reservoir extends by about 200 metres into the eastern sector of the city, in the heart of which lies the actual temple complex. This extensive area between the outer wall and the moat and walls of the inner temple, which covers 448 hectares, now includes only eight single-chambered shrines, but presumably at one time it would have housed a considerable population.

The walls of the inner sanctum are covered in bas-reliefs revealing battle scenes between the Khmer and the Chams. There is a naval battle and an army on the march, with leaders riding their elephants. On one occasion, the troops stop in front of a large forest filled with monkeys. We can see the baggage train with elephants and military supplies. The reliefs also include *apsaras* and an extraordinary range of gods with multiple heads and arms.

A maze of shrines and passageways cluster round the central temple. An inscription describes how it held an image of Srindrakumaraputra, the crown prince who led a successful expedition against Champa. He predeceased his father and was represented here as Lokesvara with the name Srindradeva. It is entirely possible that this was his funerary mausoleum. Four of his followers are also commemorated, each occupying a corner of the sanctuary. Arjunadeva lies to the south-east, Dharadevapuradeva to the north-east, Devadeva to the south-west and Varddhanadeva to the north-west. According to the text, King Yashovarman II was confronted by a rebellion, probably some sort of peasant revolt in the difficult times following the Cham assault on Angkor in 1177. Arjunadeva and Dharadevapuradeva died defending the king. They were given their own temples at Banteay Chmar, together with high posthumous titles, and their families were rewarded with gifts. The other two warriors died defending the king during a battle against the Chams, and were likewise provided with a hero's funeral and high posthumous titles.

When Jayavarman VII died *circa* 1219, he had endowed an Angkor that he and his contemporaries would still recognize. The waters of the Jayatataka might have dried up, but the Neak Pean temple still stands. The walls and entrances to Angkor Thom remain, but the vibrant bustle of city life has now given way to forest. The serene faces on the Bayon still look into the distance, albeit now the colour of sandstone rather than gold. Even his roads and bridges survive, and the ruins of his hospitals and rest houses remain as a testament to the greatest builder in the history of Angkor.

The reaction after the reign of Jayavarman VII

We do not know the exact date of Jayavarman VII's death, nor the degree to which his building projects were continued by his successor, Indravarman II. There was certainly a reduction in the number of inscriptions and a virtual cessation in the construction of new monumental buildings, although Jacques has suggested that the temples of Prasat Suor Prat and the walls that encircle Ta Prohm and Banteay Kdei were built during the reign of Indravarman II. This king, who continued the preference for Buddhism, died in 1243.

King Jayavarman VIII was a Shivaite and iconoclast who destroyed or modified every image of the Buddha he could lay his hands on, including the great statue that had graced the Bayon. Many smaller shrines at the Bayon were swept away and the site was modified to become a temple to Shiva. At Preah Khan, the images of Buddha set in wall niches were taken away and on Neak Pean, a Buddha image was converted into a *linga*. At the four temples at the corners of Angkor Thom, Buddhas were transformed into *lingas* and at Preah Khan, images of Buddha were turned into those of ascetics.

In 1295, Jayavarman VIII endowed a new temple (known today as the Mangalartha in Angkor Thom) with villages and workers, and dedicated it to the Shivaite scholar, Jayamangalartha. In order to ensure its continuity, he created a permanent and hereditary priestly office to the cult. Although this is the only major new temple known from this reign, Jayavarman VIII was responsible for much embellishment of older buildings as well as the zealous defacement of the Buddhist shrines of his two predecessors. The decorated walls round the ornamental ponds north of the Phimeanakas, for example, date from his reign, and much effort was expended to enlarge and decorate the terrace of the leper king.

In this same year, or perhaps a year later, Jayavarman VIII was the victim of a palace coup and the throne was taken by his son-in-law under the name of Indravarman III. About seventy or eighty years had now elapsed since the death of Jayavarman VII and the period so vividly portrayed on the reliefs of the Bayon. Little is known about the reign of Indravarman III, although the second phase of cremation burials at Sras Srang dates to the second half of the thirteenth century. Grave goods associated with the burial jars included an iron sword, a spearhead, a dagger with a shell haft, bronze images of Buddha and rings and hooks for palanquins.

In the year 1296, however, we obtain a priceless glimpse of life at Angkor, as seen through the eyes of a Chinese diplomat.

An ambassador visits Angkor

Zhou Daguan was a member of a diplomatic mission to Cambodia. He arrived in August 1296 and stayed for eleven months as a guest in a house in Angkor Thom, so he was able to observe life in the capital at his leisure. After his return to China, he wrote an account of his visit, which illuminates many hidden corners of life in the city and countryside. This has survived in the Chinese archives and was first translated into French exactly 493 years later.

We can follow his path and recognize the landmarks he described. The city, he said, was, surrounded by high walls and a moat crossed by five causeways bordered by fifty-four giants holding a serpent 'as if it were trying to escape'. Beyond lay enormous gates surmounted by five stone heads, one of which was covered in gold. The gates were closed every night and opened again in the morning. Dogs and criminals who had had their toes cut off were barred entry. The centre of the city was dominated by the tower of gold (the Bayon). Nearby lay the tower of bronze (the Baphuon), which rose even higher than the tower of gold. The royal palace lay to the north, and another golden tower, the Phimeanakas, rose above the surrounding walls. To the east, a golden bridge flanked by gilded lions led to a pavilion supported by stone elephants. This must be the elephant terrace.

Zhou Daguan then described the stone tower (the Bakheng), just south of the main gate, and, at some distance further south, the temple of Angkor Wat. In the middle of the Jayatataka, he says, was an island with a golden temple, many small shrines, and an elephant, bull and horse in bronze. The eastern lake contained a stone temple with a bronze Buddha from which water cascaded through its navel. Briggs maintains that Zhou Daguan mistook the Eastern for the Western Baray, where a bronze statue of

Vishnu has been found, and it is intriguing that he did not mention a third major reservoir.

From a social point of view, it is particularly interesting to note his observations on city life. Houses of the higher class were roofed with tiles and were oriented in the same direction, but the homes of the lower classes were roofed with thatch. The royal palace was set apart by its own walls and guards. Between 1000 and 2000 women who worked there could be recognized by a particular hairstyle. Living outside the royal precinct, they would pass in and out to undertake their duties. We are allowed a glimpse of life in a middle-class home, perhaps that in which Zhou Daguan lived for nearly a year. The floor is covered by matting, but there are no tables, chairs or beds. Rice is husked in a mortar and cooked in a ceramic vessel over a clay stove supported by three stones. Doubtless it was charged with charcoal. Members of the family sit on mats and eat from ceramic or copper plates. A half-coconut is used as a ladle, and small cups are made from leaves to contain sauces. They also use leaves to soak up the juices. They drink wine, made from honey, rice, leaves and water, from tin cups, although nobles use silver or gold, and the lower classes, pottery.

Everyone slept on mats laid out on the floor, but the climate was so hot that people even rose during the night to bathe. Two or three families would cooperate to dig a ditch for use as a latrine, and cover it with leaves. When it was full, they would dig another, although this may have been one of the duties of the slaves. Apparently, rich families would maintain over 100 slaves, while poorer families had only a handful or none at all. These slaves, whilst able to speak Khmer, were acquired from the forested uplands. Recaptured slaves who had attempted to escape were confined by an iron collar or anklet.

Life in the city was punctuated with religious festivals, when crowds gathered on the open ground beside the royal palace for parades, firework displays, or to watch boar or elephant fighting. The king and his court would on occasion take their place on the reviewing stand to watch the proceedings. Zhou Daguan also described the twelve small towers, the Prasat Suor Prat, opposite this parade ground. He said that when two families disputed over an issue, a member of each would be confined within one of these towers and, when they were released, guilt would be determined by the physical effects suffered, whether a fever or other ailment. The king was the ultimate arbiter in legal matters, and punishments included fines, mutilation, or crushing of one of the limbs.

There were specialized astronomers who could predict eclipses, and establishments where scribes would prepare petitions. The inspector for the collection of live human gall lived near the northern gate. Until recently gall had been used to give courage to men and elephants. The former drank it mixed with wine; the latter had a concoction poured over their heads. There was also a cosmopolitan element to the city. Zhou Daguan noted the number of Chinese immigrants, who had been attracted by the climate and the ease with which one could find a house and a wife and engage in commerce. There was a vigorous demand for Chinese goods, from blue porcelain to saltpetre, including lacquerware, hemp cloth, iron and copper vessels, sieves and wooden combs. Women excelled in trade, and would sell their wares in a market from a mat placed on the ground, having paid a rent to the local authorities.

He noted three groups of religious functionaries, with Buddhism being dominant. The Buddhist monks had shaven heads and wore a yellow robe that covered their right shoulders. Their followers supplied them with one meal a day, and they chanted from texts set down on neatly folded palm leaves. They eat meat and fish, he says, but do not drink wine. Some senior monks had palanquins and might be consulted by the king on serious issues. The other two religious groups were probably Brahmans and Shivaites.

Zhou Daguan must have ventured beyond the city, for he described the annual agricultural round, beginning with the contrast between the wet and the dry seasons. The rice farmers employed ploughs, sickles and hoes, but did not use cattle as draught animals. Although he did not specifically mention it, it is likely that water buffalo were used to draw the plough, as they are to this day. In one passage, which has caused some controversy, he noted that the people manage three or four harvests a year. They also grew a wide variety of vegetables, such as mustard, onions and taro, and many different fruits: oranges, plums and bananas. Horses, sheep, goats, cattle, pigs and water buffaloes were all domesticated.

The kingdom was divided into ninety provinces, each with a governor who lived in a centre defended by wooden palisades. Such defences were vital in the light of a recent war that he reported, against the Siamese. Much transport was effected by boats, built of planks of wood secured with iron nails, but there were also roads, furnished at intervals with rest houses. Palanquins transported grandees, but for long distances people used elephants and horses. Beyond the lowland rice fields and orchards lay the forest, with its many varieties of scented wood and resin. Here, the local inhabitants sought kingfisher feathers, and hunted elephant and rhinoceros for ivory and the valued horn.

Zhou Daguan was a member of a mission sent by the Chinese emperor, and was therefore able to enter the royal precinct to experience the audiences given twice daily by the king. The supplicants first heard distant music, and then trumpets heralded the arrival of the king who was revealed at a golden window, holding the sacred golden sword, as two women pulled back a curtain. Everyone linked hands and prostrated themselves, touching the ground with their foreheads and only raising their heads when the trumpets ceased. The king alone wore clothing finely woven with floral patterns, as well as a gold diadem, bracelets, anklets and finger rings of gold. His necklace was made up of countless pearls.

A royal progress beyond the palace involved a procession headed by a cavalry escort with pennants, standards and music. Three to five hundred beautifully dressed women of the palace followed holding burning tapers, and then a group of women carrying gold and silver vessels. The female palace guards were next, armed with swords and shields. Ministers and princes ranged behind them, each riding an elephant and surrounded by a forest of gold and silver parasols. Zhou Daguan set down their titles: *mratan* had the gold parasols, *sresthin* the silver. The king's concubines took their turn, riding in palanquins, wheeled carriages or on elephants. Last was the king himself on a massive elephant with gilded tusks, holding the sacred sword and shaded by twenty parasols. His elephant was surrounded by many others, which pressed round him for protection. The costs of the court and administration were still met by taxes: an inscription from Angkor Thom sets out the amounts due.

This scene differs little from the depiction at Angkor Wat of the procession of Suryavarman II. If we move forward in time to May 1901, it is possible to find later echoes in the ceremonial cutting of the hair of Prince Chandalekha, son of King Norodom, when he came of age. The procession included: members of the royal lineage whose ancestry could be traced back for several centuries; mandarins dressed in the costume of angels with clothes bordered with cloth of gold; and women of the palace bearing the royal insignia, among which are a sword, a large fan, a spitoon and a box for betel. The young prince was borne aloft on a palanquin shaded with parasols and wore cloth of gold, heavy gold anklets and a gold ornament encrusted with diamonds. At the palace, King Norodom waited on a raised pavilion shaded by parasols, as eight dancing girls holding peacock plumes danced in honour of Shiva. A royal retainer at Suryavarman's court would have felt quite at home.

After Zhou Daguan

For the period following Zhou Daguan's memoirs, we must rely upon a small and diminishing number of inscriptions. Indrajayavarman succeeded Indravarman III in 1308 and ruled for nineteen years. A text from Prasat Kombot in the lower Chinit River valley still referred to Angkor as Yashodharapura. It is a Buddhist inscription, which ponders the problems of rebirth into new existences based on merit and the dangers of punishment for the sinful.

The most important text from this shadowy period comes from the temple of Mangalartha in Angkor Thom. It records the history, since the reign of Jayavarman VII, of a noble family that was founded when the Burmese scholar, Sri Jaya Mahapradhana, settled in Angkor and became the royal chaplain. He continued in this role under Indravarman II, and we learn that on the death of the latter, he went to the Shivaite shrine at Bhimapura (Phimai) to pray for the king's soul. There, he met and married a virtuous and educated woman called Sriprabha. They had six children, one of whom, Cakravartirajadevi, married King Jayavarman VIII. One of their sons founded the temple in which this inscription was to be placed. Sriprabha's sister, Subhadra, married the savant and Shivaite scholar, Jayamangalartha Suri. King Jayavarman VIII greatly admired this professor who lived to the age of 104, and erected statues to him and his mother, which were dedicated in 1295. He also founded a shrine dedicated to them both, deified under the names Sri Jaya Trivikrama-Mahanatha and Sri Jaya Trivikrama-Devesvari. This foundation received by royal favour gold and silver vessels, three villages, workers, dancers and singers, and a hereditary cult priesthood in perpetuity. The temple was further enriched by kings Indravarman III and Indrajaya-varman, and it was during the reign of the latter, which began in 1308, that the inscription was set up. The endowment of such a foundation by royal patronage with land and goods, the erection of images to great ancestors and the detailed recording of family histories clearly continued well into the fourteenth century at Angkor.

Jayavarmaparamesvara came to the throne in 1327. A severely fragmented text calls him Shiva incarnate, and cites the foundation of a hermitage dedicated to Shiva. It also hints at unrest and conflict. This is the last Sanskrit inscription to come from the civilization of Angkor, and is notable not only for what it says, but for the excellent quality of its verse; scholarship was still thriving.

The lack of building activity and the erection of inscriptions severely impairs our knowledge of the last years of Angkor as a continuously occupied capital. We know from various later sources, however, that warfare became endemic as the power of the Siamese centred at Ayutthaya increased, and that in 1430–1 Angkor was sacked by the Siamese after a long siege. The political centre of Cambodia then moved back to where it had been seven centuries previously, athwart the Mekong River. It is recorded in Cambodian annals that the king of Siam removed many statues of the Buddha to his own court at Ayutthaya. These in turn were taken by the conquering Burmese in 1569 to Pegu, whence in 1734 they were transported to Mandalay. They can still be seen there. Angkor Thom, the capital city of Jayavarman VII, was then overtaken by the forest.

Angkor is rediscovered by the West

A century and a half elapsed since the abandonment of Angkor before the Portuguese reported legends of how a King Satha, on his elephant hunt, encountered its great stone walls and moved his court there. Bartolome de Argensola wrote in 1609:

> One finds in the interior within inaccessible forests, a city of six thousand houses, called Angon. The monuments and roads are made of marble, and are intact. The sculptures are also intact, as if they were modern. There is a strong wall. The moat, stone lined, can admit boats. The bridges are supported by stone giants. Where the canals end, one sees the vestiges of gardens. The perimeter of a lake in the area surpasses 30 leagues. There are epitaphs, inscriptions, which have not been deciphered. And in all this city, the natives discovered it, there were no people, no animals, nothing living. I confess I hesitate to write this, it appears as fantastic as the Atlantis of Plato. Today the city is uninhabited. A learned man supposed these to be the works of Trajan.

The Cambodians, however, never doubted that Angkor Wat was built by the king's ancestors. Indeed, circa 1550, further reliefs were carved on its walls and it continued to attract Buddhist pilgrims. One of their number, a Japanese, visited the temple in the early seventeenth century and made a map with descriptive notes, which survive in a 1715 copy. He even described the gods pulling on a rope, a clear reference to the scene showing the churning of the ocean of milk. In 1668 Father Chevreuil, a French missionary, wrote of Angkor Wat as being renowned by the people of South-East Asia. In 1789, the first translation of Zhou Daguan's memoir was published in Paris, and from 1850 there was a regular flow of Western visitors, including Father Charles-Emile Bouillevaux and the biologist-explorer, Henri Mouhot. The first photographs of Angkor Wat, taken by John Thomson in 1866, show a well-maintained temple with occupied Buddhist buildings in the foreground. Two years previously, Cambodia had become, by treaty, a French protectorate, setting in train French domination of the study and restoration of the monuments. This process quickened with the establishment of the French School of the Far East (the École Française d'Extrême-Orient). While the temples were cleared of the jungle, many statues were uplifted and taken to France. New inscriptions were uncovered and translated, and piece by piece, the dynastic sequence and history of Angkor were revealed.

This process of restoration and maintenance continued during the Second World War, and was strengthened when in 1953 Cambodia achieved independence. The nightmare of the Khmer Rouge, however, brought all work to a halt and extreme concern over the fate of the great monuments was widely felt. Fortunately, apart from the occasional bullet scar, Angkor survived relatively unscathed and with the return of peace, it has again opened its doors to tourism. The visitor today will find that the restoration continues: the Baphuon is shrouded in scaffolding, and parts of the Bayon are closed to visitors. Nevertheless, it is still possible to find an isolated corner of Ta Prohm as dusk falls, when the bats make their evening appearance, and allow the mind to wander over the descriptive passages in the foundation stela of a host of priests, dancers and devotees. The view over the Eastern Mebon from the summit of Pre Rup can still bring forth an image of the sacred waters of the Yashodharatataka as they mirrored the bright stucco temple on its island sanctuary.

The past century of research on these monuments and inscriptions, however, still represents only the first step in the Western understanding of this civilization of Angkor, a journey that is far from finished.

CHAPTER 8

THE CIVILIZATION OF ANGKOR

The civilization of Angkor was established on the northern shore of the Great Lake in Cambodia, and progressively controlled the Mekong Valley to the delta, the Khorat plateau of north-east Thailand and much of central Thailand. Its origins and develop-ment can now be traced through four distinct phases, beginning about 500 BC in the prehistoric Iron Age. The second phase saw a swift transition to the state of Funan in the Mekong Delta, fuelled by participation in a burgeoning international trade network. During the sixth century, trading patterns altered and the delta was bypassed. The focus of social change moved inland, to the river valleys feeding the Mekong between the upper delta and Pakse. For 250 years from AD 550, a series of competing kings vied for supremacy. One leader, Jayavarman I, achieved sufficient central power to form, recognizably, an inland, agrarian state. This was the background for Jayavarman II, in the last decades of the eighth century, to lay the foundations for the state of Angkor, which was to dominate mainland South-East Asia until the fifteenth century.

  How and why did this great civilization develop, and how does it compare with other pre-industrial states that flourished in similarly hot, lowland conditions?

Phase 1: the prehistoric Iron Age

The ultimate foundation for Angkor was laid when, over 4000

143

years ago, small communities of rice farmers travelling down the main rivers of South-East Asia from the north brought settled village life. These people probably spoke a language ancestral to the Khmer spoken today in Cambodia. Between 1500 and 1000 BC, these farmers learnt how to smelt copper and tin, probably through contact with the civilizations of China. They valued exotic ornaments of marble, slate and marine shell in their mortuary rituals, while large copper mines and processing sites reflect their increasing interest in the casting of bronzes. Recent research into the Iron Age, which was under way by 500 BC, has revealed a picture totally at variance with previous pronouncements that these indigenous people were at best backward savages who gratefully accepted the benefits of Indian civilization, or at worst cowering natives who had no answer to Indian colonization. Iron has the potential to stimulate major economic and social change. The ore is widely available, and excavations at several sites have revealed how it was employed. The earliest burials at Noen U-Loke in the Mun Valley, which date to about 400–300 BC, included offerings made from iron. A woman was interred with neck rings and bangles, a man with a large socketed spear or dagger and a hoe. Already, we can recognize the use of iron for ornaments, in conflict and probably in agriculture. In due course, spades and sickles reveal further improvements in agricultural technology, while arrowheads and spears proliferated. This evidence for conflict, seen in an arrowhead lodged in a man's spine, should be placed in its regional context: settlement sites were up to ten times larger than in the preceding Bronze Age, and they were densely packed together.

These people chose to live in the swampy lowlands adjacent to rivers with multiple channels, some of which flowed immediately past their settlements. It is possible that the iron spades were used to control the course of these rivers by linking them to channels that enclosed the entire settlement. Certainly, the swampy lowlands would have attracted rice cultivation, and surpluses were used in mortuary rituals, to provide both a bed and a cover for the corpse within a clay-lined coffin.

Exposure of these graves at Noen U-Loke and Non Muang Kao has revealed specific clusters of interments and association of the dead with rich offerings. Bronzes were particularly abundant, in the form of bangles, ear discs, finger and toe rings, belts and head ornaments ending in graceful spirals. Tin and copper were imported from the mines in central Thailand, and were locally cast. Exotic carnelian and agate were used for beads and pendants. Iron Age leaders wore gold and silver beads and ear coils. Fine ceramic vessels, so thin that specialists were probably required in their manufacture, were filled with fish and placed with the dead. Glass beads were imported or even locally manufactured. Women were skilled in weaving cloth, some of which has survived next to iron grave goods. These large settlements also provide evidence for structures, probably houses, with plastered floors and wooden walls.

The excavations of Noen U-Loke and Non Muang Kao have illuminated a society that obtained many exotic items by trade, and used them in their mortuary rituals. Some of the gold and agate ornaments are very similar to those found in contemporary sites in the Mekong Delta area. Salt could have been a major trade item, and doubtless there were others. Together with a rising population and increasing inter-group tension and conflict, there are compelling grounds for a level of social complexity which, in other regions of the world, presaged the transition to the state.

Evidence for such complex and powerful Iron Age communities is not confined to the Mun Valley. In central Thailand, the site of Ban Don Ta Phet has yielded many iron weapons and exotic mortuary goods, including carnelian ornaments and paper-thin decorated bronze bowls imported from India. In the lower Mekong Valley, Iron Age settlements are responding to excavation, even under the great city of Angkor Borei. Along the coast of Vietnam, a series of cemeteries has been ascribed to the Sa Huynh culture. Here, the dead were cremated and the ashes, with rich mortuary offerings, were placed in large ceramic jars. The Red River valley, until the arrival of Han Chinese colonial armies, was home to chiefs whose bronze specialists cast ceremonial drums. Some of these were traded not only on the mainland, but across the sea to Indonesia and New Guinea. Similarly, traders from the mainland made regular journeys to the Philippines.

Research into these Iron Age societies has demonstrated that they possessed increasing technical skills, an interest in trade and the ability to maintain specialists. Those occupying the coast had also inherited sufficient experience in open-sea voyaging to embark on long-distance maritime trading expeditions.

Phase 2: the delta state, AD 150–550

There are three sources of evidence for the formation of a delta trading state: archaeology, inscriptions and eye-witness accounts. Recent excavations have greatly expanded the archaeological evidence, which formerly relied almost entirely upon research at Oc Eo during the Second World War. The occupation of Angkor Borei, for example, reaches back into the Iron Age, and reveals a major phase of occupation between AD 100 and 600. Although the brick temple foundations, walls, moats and reservoirs there have yet to be dated, radiocarbon determinations from related brick structures in the delta region fall within the fifth or sixth centuries. These large walled centres were linked by a system of canals, which might have been used for drainage during the seasonal floods and to facilitate transport. Brick shrines of the same period have yielded images of Indic gods, particularly Vishnu, both as stone statues and on gold plaques. Several such plaques have been recovered from burials in which the dead were cremated and the ashes, together with grave goods, placed in a brick-lined vault.

This archaeological evidence strikes a chord with the third-century account of two Chinese emissaries. They described cities, palaces and kings, a system of taxation, writing and rice agriculture. Rulers had the title *fan*, which is probably the same word as *pon*, found in later inscriptions when referring to high-status leaders. Fan Shih Man was one such leader who expanded his domain through force of arms and placed his younger relatives in positions of authority over dependent settlements. He also commanded sea-borne raids against rivals, but it is not known precisely where these battles took place. Further friction involved regular disputes over the succession.

Early writing took the form of brief Sanskrit engravings on seals and ornaments, its style belonging to the late first or early second centuries AD. Traditional techniques were applied to the casting of ornaments, and the range of precious or semi-precious metals and gemstones indicates a far-flung trade network. This extended westward to India, Persia and the Roman empire, and eastward to China. Most surviving trade items are relatively light and small, such as coinage, glass and carnelian, but these items must represent only a fractional proportion of what must have been a much larger trade in perishable exports such as feathers, spices, fabrics and wood. There is no reason to doubt that local sailors and local ships were involved.

The first few inscriptions in stone date from the late fifth century. Their language was Sanskrit, and they describe acts of religious merit by kings who had by now adopted Indic names, such as Jayavarman and Rudravarman. The names combine that of an Indic god or a desirable attribute with the term -varman, which means shield or protector. One inscription records a victory over a rival king; another mentions a kingdom wrested from the mud, perhaps alluding to swamp drainage to facilitate agriculture. The potential for flood-retreat agriculture in this flat deltaic landscape could well have produced the rice surpluses necessary for the development of the state.

There are several variables in this picture, which are matched by historically documented changes. When, for example, we compare the sequence in the delta with that in Malawi during the nineteenth century, it is seen that the control of trade and coercive power stimulated rapid social change. Rulers in this region adopted an exotic script and religion, borrowed Arab names, built their palaces in a foreign style and encouraged agricultural intensification as their capitals expanded. By borrowing and adapting new titles, rites and symbols of status, the rulers were establishing an elite ruling class in place of the old system of kinship ties.

For at least two millennia, the prehistoric inhabitants of South-East Asia had been exchanging valuables. The new opportunities provided by growing international trade, now involving new products and ideas, are seen as a vital contributor to the rapid transition evident in the archaeological record of the delta.

This trend was not confined to the Mekong Delta. Similar changes were taking place up the coast of Vietnam among the Chams and in central Thailand, where the state was named Dvaravati. In strategic locations in peninsular Thailand and Malaysia, trading ports rapidly formed, and on Java too, we find the early development of states. All depended for their survival upon a steady flow of trading vessels. When in the sixth century new sea lanes developed that bypassed the Mekong Delta, Oc Eo was abandoned, the power of the delta kings withered and the political centre of gravity moved inland, to the flood plain of the Mekong River and its tributaries.

Phase 3: Chenla: state formation in the Mekong Valley, AD 550–800

The Chinese used the name Chenla when referring to the states that formed in the interior of Cambodia. There are many brick, single-celled temples dating from the period AD 550–800 which reveal that the lowlands bordering the Mekong and Mun valleys and the Tonle Sap witnessed deep-seated cultural changes. Most are located in the vicinity of good rice land, others are also sited to control passage up and down the major rivers. Inscriptions have provided sufficient information to construct a skeletal framework of social and economic information, although our understanding of the period remains in the exploratory stage, particularly in the near-absence of any excavations to unravel the nature of the settlements of which the temples alone survive above ground.

There is no evidence that the area in question was ever brought under the control of one king. On the contrary, the inscriptions record many rulers, some of whom were contemporaries in different regions. There was, however, one dynasty that can be traced over seven or eight generations, even if some of its leaders are known to us only as names. Sarvabhauma was father of Viravarman, whose son Bhavarvarman probably ruled from a base in the valley of the Sen River north-east of the Great Lake. He was described as the overlord of a ruler at Indrapura named Narasimhagupta. His brother Mahendravarman led raids up the Mekong to its junction with the Mun River, and westward up the Mun River valley, leaving brief Sanskrit inscriptions claiming victories as he went. Mahendravarman's son Ishanavarman I established a most impressive capital at Ishanapura, which is dominated by clusters of shrines within brick-walled enclosures. Inscriptions describe him as a successful military leader who expanded the domain of his parents. He sent one of his sons to rule at Jyesthapura to the west. The ruler of Tamrapura acknowledged vassal status to Ishanavarman, but at the same time is said to have been in a position of authority over three other settlements. At least three tiers of settlement hierarchy are suggested, from the capital to dependent centres. As far as 250 kilometres south of Ishanapura, a local leader referred to Ishanavarman in glowing terms.

There are also inscriptions dating to Ishanavarman's reign that do not mention him. Indeed, removed from the capital, much authority was vested in local leaders entitled *pon*, who had the authority to endow community temples with land and livestock, and assign the necessary people to supply and maintain services. So we encounter musicians, dancers, cooks, leaf sewers and, probably, blacksmiths. Most temple servants worked in the rice fields and no doubt in the creation of the many reservoirs that dotted the landscape. There is only the most tenuous evidence for any form of irrigation, but water was essential for the maintenance of communities through the dry season. It is likely that most of the workers during this period were junior kin of the community leaders, and that the gods they worshipped, despite the Indic veneer, were ancestral spirits. Leadership was passed down from the *pon* to his sister's son, a system probably with deep prehistoric roots that continued for centuries among noble families. This presented an obstacle to the accumulation of wealth and power in elite hands, since wealth accumulated by an individual would be inherited by his nephews. It also militated against the assurance of a peaceful dynastic succession, as a king with many wives could sire sufficient sons to ensure conflicting claims to the throne.

Ishanavarman's immediate successors are shadowy figures about whom little is known, but his great-grandson, Jayavarman I, fundamentally changed the central and regional administration, with *pon*, whose position was hereditary, declining at the expense of appointed officials known as *mratan*. He created new posts and titles, rewarding loyalty with high-status symbols, such as the coveted white parasol; there was a chief of the elephants, a person in charge of levying tax and probably also a chief of grain stores. It was probably the king who issued orders regulating the river transport of salt. Taxation and commercial transactions now and throughout the Angkorian period (from AD 800) involved surplus production of commodities such as rice, cloth and oil. Some inscriptions also refer to measures of gold and silver, but there was no system of currency. Jayavarman I appointed a governor of Dhruvapura, and then moved this official to Dhanvipura, placing him in command of 1000 soldiers. Indeed, war was often mentioned in his inscriptions.

We lose sight of this dynasty in the early years of the eighth century, at a time when inscriptions became rare. This change has often been cited as evidence for the break-up of a unified state and the start of a period of fragmentation and strife. This, however, is most unlikely. Even in its heyday, the kingdom of Jayavarman I never encompassed all of Cambodia, and his reign was disturbed by warfare. During the eighth century, a polity based at Sambhupura was ruled by three successive queens; a series of kings with the title *-aditya* (rising sun) is known for central Cambodia; and in the Mun Valley we read of at least five generations of kings in the polity of Canasapura. The rise and fall of small kingdoms is not unusual during periods of state formation.

These 250 years were seminal in the formation of the kingdom of Angkor, for under Ishanavarman, and particularly his great-grandson Jayavarman I, steps were taken to found an agrarian state based on central control over land and labour. It is possible to identify several key innovations and to assess their interactions. The king occupied the central position in ritual mediation with the gods. Kings were given the divine titles of gods after their deaths; in the case of Jayavarman, while he was still alive. The old system of local leadership by *pon* was replaced by central appointments, and during the reign of Jayavarman, high state officials were authorized, royal orders were sent down to the provinces, officials were given provincial responsibilities and punishment was decreed against those transgressing royal orders. The king increasingly controlled manpower both for production and war. In the right hands, these innovations could be welded into a larger and still more powerful kingdom.

Phase 4: the capital at Angkor, AD 800–1432

The fourth phase saw the establishment of capitals on the plain between the Tonle Sap and the Kulen plateau. There were at least two, and probably three, dynasties and much warfare. Despite fundamental changes during these six centuries, there is also an underlying continuity.

The capital was the religious and ritual centre of the kingdom, and it radiated spiritual power. Jayavarman II was consecrated in a ceremony on the sacred mountain of Mahendraparvata, during which he was declared supreme ruler. His loyal followers were rewarded with grants of land, and court titles and duties. Two centuries later, the descendants of these officials, now related by blood to the royal family, jealously protected their estates and privileges after a ruinous civil war. After another two centuries, Jayavarman VII had his image as Jayabuddhamahanatha placed in Angkor and major provincial centres. The state was centred on a king imbued with divinity, who had around him a corps of aristocratic officials and advisers. In theory, the provinces, through a network of state and family temples, donated sufficient consumables and treasures to sustain not only the administration, but the ritual needs of the gods.

The king had the right to donate land to faithful retainers and to confiscate it from his enemies. Expansion into new territory, such as the Mun Valley, may have changed little, other than according the local overlord a title, high-status gifts and binding him in loyalty to the centre. A land grant was usually followed by the foundation of a family or lineage temple, together with priests, reservoirs, animals and workers. By investing capital in the form of buffaloes and cattle, seed and ploughs, the owners brought new land into production, a proportion of which was donated to a state temple.

It is very difficult to pin down the status of the workers. Some could be bought and sold, some were war captives, while others may well have been in the service of the noble family for generations and were assigned to develop a new foundation. Tied labour is not unusual in South-East Asia. As recently as the Ayutthaya period in Thailand, which ended in the eighteenth century, workers were tattooed to record their assigned place of work and to maintain a stable workforce. There are reminders of this in the inscription from Phnom Kanva, Battambang, which describes how Viruna, a worker who had escaped from the estate where he was born, had his eyes gouged out and his nose cut off. It was also customary in listing workers to include their children and even grandchildren. Workers are often listed as being responsible for either the fifteen dark or the fifteen light days of each month on a rota system, and could work on land assigned to them, according to one text, in their own time.

The temple inscriptions represent a tiny fraction of the archives. It is important to avoid the pitfall of assuming that the state was preoccupied only with religious matters, important as they were. The inscriptions also refer to war, albeit in terms of fulsome royal eulogies, and occasionally mention trade or foreign goods. There are, for example, references to Chinese silks, mosquito nets and ceramics. As soon as alternative sources of information are available, whether from archaeological excavation, the bas-reliefs of the Bayon or the account of Zhou Daguan, it is possible to appreciate the quantity of Chinese trade wares. We can see images of a Chinese trading junk and the interior of a Chinese merchant's house. Zhou Daguan described many Chinese traders who had settled at Angkor, and visited the market place. It is not known if the royal treasury was augmented by customs dues, but it is clear that the people of Angkor were not sealed off from outside contact.

Angkorian society also contained far more facets than its ruling elite and its temple workers. Only occasionally, inscriptions mention expert craftsmen, like the corporation of goldsmiths. But there must have been many specialists just to cast the bronze palanquin fitments and figurines, let alone the huge statues, such as Vishnu from the Western Mebon. The recently discovered concentration of stoneware kilns at Tani, 20 kilometres from Angkor, and the better-known concentration at Ban Kruat in Thailand, indicate the existence of full-time potters. There must also have been a major salt-making industry, and boatbuilders for the barges that plied the Mekong. Blacksmiths, weavers, traders and miners do not emerge from the inscriptions, but their output leaves no doubt as to their presence.

Over such a lengthy period, the titles and the number of officials changed. Under Rajendravarman and Jayavarman V, there was the *rajakulamahamantri*, a great adviser. There were numerous grades of officials charged with control over royal warehouses, the payment of taxes, the administration of land boundaries, the command of the army and the organization of corvée labour.

Kings who ruled for a significant period of time would have a state temple constructed, initially in the form of a raised pyramid to house a *linga* named after themselves and Shiva, which embodied the power of the state. The temple represented Mount Meru, the home of the Hindu gods, just as the walls and moats symbolized the surrounding mountains and oceans. Kings put in place divinized images of their ancestors, whose names were again subtly combined with those of the gods, and worshipped them. With the king's death, this temple became his mausoleum. Ideologically, the linking of the central and regional temples into a devotional web in which endowments, worship and loyalty brought merit to accumulate for the next rebirth was a strong bonding mechanism.

The re-creation of heaven on earth and the pursuit of ideological perfection ran counter to human frailties. One of the recurrent problems faced by the rulers of Angkor was a centrifugal tendency, in which outlying areas paid only lip service to central edicts. A second weakness was factionalism in the centre. Suryavarman I appears to have attempted to exert a centralizing authority over the semi-independent princes living north of the Dang Raek range. Three decades after his death, the princely dynasty of Mahidharapura rose in revolt and, in the person of Jayavarman VI, took Angkor. The lack of firm rules of succession, linked with the practice of polygamy and the ancient tradition of descent through the female line, meant that any number of princes could claim a legitimate title. Suryavarman himself, for example, claimed descent from the line of Indravarman I when he deposed Jayaviravarman. Even Indravarman avoided direct reference to his two predecessors in the ninth century. In the case of Indravarman III, possession of the *preah khan*, the sacred sword and symbol of kingship, secured him the throne at the expense of his father-in-law. Instability thus lay at the core and at the outer reaches of the civilization of Angkor.

Given the scale of Angkor as it expanded and changed over the centuries, it is tempting to concentrate attention on the centre at the expense of the countryside. Virtually no archaeological research has been undertaken beyond Angkor. Even great temples like Beng Mealea and Preah Khan of Kompong Svay lie virtually untouched.

Rice was the solid foundation of this civilization, and the way in which it was produced is a vital but controversial issue. Rural village life today is the best illustration of the underlying seasonal rhythms. In Thailand, the Bang Fai festival in May calls on the spirits to bring rain. Huge rockets in the shape of a *linga* are fired into the clouds to fertilize them. Already, low-lying nursery beds near streams and swamps are emerald green with rice destined to be transplanted. As the first rain clouds sweep up from the south-west, softening the rock-hard soil, the men hitch buffaloes to the ploughshares and turn the soil, then harrow the furrows to produce the soft, creamy tilth in which the rice will take root. In the main fields, each plant is transplanted by women, a back-breaking task but one that will bring higher yields than broadcasting seed. Steady rains over the ensuing months will assure good returns, but a lull or too much rain can spell disaster as the plants either wither or drown. November and December bring the harvest, as rows of men and women with iron sickles cut and bind the golden heads of rice, load them onto a bullock cart and take them to the threshing floor. When the wind turns to the north-eastern quarter, the rice fields dry and crack. Streams turn into a trickle, lakes and swamps dry out. Villagers bring water for their domestic needs from the reservoir next to the temple, and go out into the now burnt rice fields to dig for crabs, or to trap rats and birds. The communities' basic survival turns on stores of rice and fish, fermented and preserved with salt.

In central and north-east Thailand today, it is possible to produce a second rice crop in favoured areas with water stored and distributed from the state dams, which are named after the king, queen and members of the royal family. In some years, water is scarce and disputes arise. If tobacco farmers illegally take water from the canal, there may not be enough for the hospital down-stream. Water is the essence of life, and as March turns into April and the temperature rises, so the return of the monsoon is awaited with growing impatience.

The agricultural regime differs markedly in the delta and the widely flooded plains surrounding the rivers and lakes. Here, there is a superabundance of water during the wet season, leading to flooding so deep that rice cultivation is not possible. However, as the water retreats in December, rice can be transplanted into soil that is replenished annually by silt. While these rice fields can be ploughed, it is not vital. It is, however, necessary to feed water into the dry-season fields from natural or artificial reservoirs, a technique that usually provides much better yields than the inundation system.

Did the kings build the great reservoirs at Angkor to irrigate rice fields? Since water is so essential, to have done so would have given them an aura of divine and supernatural power. There are two diametrically opposed schools of thought. Bernard-Philippe Groslier and Jacques Dumarçay are two French scholars who spent many years studying Angkor. Each concluded that it was an essentially hydraulic city in which the reservoirs were the source of irrigation water for the rice fields. Its location was selected because of the perennial rivers bringing water from the Kulen plateau to replenish the reservoirs and service the rice fields. Philip Stott, W. van Liere and Robert Acker, on the other hand, argue against any irrigation on technical and geographic grounds. Since the former school maintains that the rise of the Angkor state and indeed its decline and abandonment were determined by the success and failure of the irrigation system, it is important to review both sides of the debate.

There are several sources of evidence. The *barays* are very large, and contained many millions of cubic metres of water. Could they have held sufficient to make any impact upon rice agriculture in the area between their southern dyke and the Tonle Sap? Is there any evidence for a reticulation system? Are there any structures to permit the controlled egress of water from the *barays* into a network of distributaries? Was there sufficient irrigable land to contribute to the amount of rice needed to sustain the populace? (One could then seek any reference to irrigation in the inscriptions, whether in terms of named officials or disputes over water.) Finally, did Zhou Daguan describe irrigation?

Groslier emphasized that the location of Angkor provided the opportunity to control the southward flow of water. The sites for the Iron Age settlements in this area were chosen with reference to the rivers. Banteay Choeu, the first known historic centre, with its temple of Ak Yum, was located astride the Puok River. Hariharalaya commanded the Roluos River, which filled the Indratataka. Yashodharapura, he suggested, was placed to take advantage of the Siem Reap River. This was during what he described as the first phase of the hydraulic city of Angkor. The second saw the construction of the Western Baray and the third involved the building of Angkor Wat. Groslier even felt that the water in the moat round this temple added significantly to the capacity of the irrigation system. Finally, the fourth phase of the city saw the construction of the Jayatataka and the city of Angkor Thom. With each stage, the irrigated area expanded.

Dumarçay's summary builds upon this framework. The Indratataka, he claimed, began as a dyke to accumulate stream flows, but was then extended by lateral branches and completed along the northern end to prevent sedimentation. In this progressive manner, he argues, the form of a *baray* emerged and was copied with the much larger Yashodharatataka. The latter silted up so quickly that it might have contributed to the abandonment of Angkor for Lingapura. Yet, on his return to Yashodharapura, Rajendravarman found the *baray* still filled with water after an interval of 60 years, as indeed it still was, according to an inscription, in the reign of Jayavarman V. However, the Western Baray was constructed by Suryavarman I together with a central temple with a *linga* connected to the waters of the *baray* by a cylindrical tunnel. As the level of the water rose, so the *linga* filled with water, symbolizing its fertilizing power. The war with the Chams had so damaged the irrigation system, says Dumarçay, that Jayavarman VII overhauled it with the construction of the Jayatataka. Instead of relying on gravity to allow water to spread into the rice fields, he made use 'of bridges which acted as dams that could be closed or opened according to irrigation needs. This transformation was radical, for ... canals had to be dug to bring water where it was required, and more seriously, this dispersal of the water reserves caused a weakening of the central power which derived from the control of the distribution of water.' This survey is unreferenced, making it impossible to check the sources for these various claims.

From the beginning of *baray* construction, Khmer builders regulated the flow of water into canals and moats. The first city of Yashodharapura was crossed by linked canals and water basins. Angkor Thom incorporated stone-lined culverts to take water from interior canals to the moats beyond the city walls. If the *barays* retained irrigation water, where are the outlets and canals leading to the rice fields? Groslier responded to this question by suggesting that a channel was excavated outside and parallel with the southern dykes, which filled with water percolating through the dyke. Van Liere, however, has shown that this is technically impossible. A *tanub* is a dyke built up parallel to the shore of the Great Lake to retain flood water. In his description of the *tanub* system of dry-season rice cultivation today, J. Delvert has noted that the distribution channels are redug annually. This might explain their absence below the *barays*, but it should be noted that the *tanub* system operates below the maximum height of the flooded Tonle Sap. All the *barays* are positioned well above this limit.

Acker has given detailed consideration to the area that could have been irrigated, the water requirement, the likely yields, and the location of the *barays* relative to each other and the land below them. He began with Groslier's own figures, which involved a population estimated (it seems very generously) as 1,900,000 people of whom 600,000 were supported by 86,000 hectares of irrigated rice fields. In the dry season, a hectare would require 15,000 cubic metres of water. Assuming that all the major *barays* at Angkor were full to a depth of 3 metres, they could have supplied 7000 hectares. At an optimistic yield of 1.46 tonnes per hectare and an annual consumption of 220 kilograms of rice per capita, the dry-season yield would have maintained about 44,500 people, just under 2.5 per cent of Groslier's estimated population. This calculation is based only on the amount of water available when the *barays* were 3 metres deep. It does not take into account the possibility that the *barays* could have been constantly replenished with water from the Siem Reap River throughout the dry season. There is also the possibility that the reservoirs were used to supplement water supplies to the fields when there was insufficient rainfall during the wet season. If so, then a further 9000 tonnes over and above anticipated wet-season production could have been obtained, bringing the total irrigated yield to 19,200 tonnes or sufficient to feed nearly 100,000 people.

These figures assume that all the *barays* were being employed simultaneously, a situation only possible during the reigns of Jayavarman VII and his successors. On the other hand, Acker has shown that the reservoirs mask each other from potentially irrigable rice fields. Similarly, the Yashodharatataka could not have irrigated all the potential land below it, because the incised channel of the Siem Reap River would have made it impossible.

The inscriptions that mention the reservoirs do not link them with irrigation. A description of an estate at Hariharalaya cites the Indratataka as a boundary marker but does not mention water. Another inscription describes Yashovarman I as the husband of the earth, who filled it with virtue, pleasure and fecundity, but the ensuing mention of his *baray* is too damaged to allow its full meaning to be obtained. His foundation inscriptions compare the Yashodharatataka to the moon, the source of life-sustaining ambrosia. Rajendravarman, it is said, filled the water with his good works, and made it a mirror to reflect his temple in the middle. There is also a description of his erecting images in this Eastern Mebon island temple, whose shrines were embellished with stucco. If Jayavarman VII had brought water to the rice fields, it would surely have appeared in his lengthy texts as one of his meritorious acts. Nor do we read anywhere of disputes over water, or of officials charged with its distribution.

Negative evidence does not prove anything, but it is nevertheless intriguing to examine a related context in Sri Lanka, where there was a centralized system of rice irrigation. The first inscriptions that describe irrigation date to the third century BC. The system seems to have begun on a small scale, with each household having a share of the irrigated land. Reservoirs were valued for their fish supply and were used for further cultivation in the dry season. Individual ownership and meritorious gifts of irrigated land to temples began during the first century AD, but it was the invention of the cistern sluice in the second century that opened the path to large-scale works. King Vasabha (AD 65–109) constructed twelve reservoirs and the Alisara canal, which took water to distant fields. By AD 150, we read of large and service reservoirs and interlocking systems. In the third century, a huge reservoir 24 kilometres in circumference was completed, and the system expanded to include twelve further reservoirs over the next five centuries. Some were royal property and built by corvée labour. Others were privately owned by people known as *vavihamika*, were in communal ownership, or were the property of monasteries. The private owners took the *dakabaka*, or water share: a proportion of the two or three crops grown annually on irrigated land. The legal system cited theft of water and fish from irrigation works as offences. No similar texts exist in Cambodia.

The only eye-witness account of agriculture in the vicinity of Angkor comes from the brush of Zhou Daguan. He wrote that three or four crops a year could be obtained, a statement that supporters of the irrigation theory take as support. On the other hand, Zhou Daguan did not specify that they all came from the same plot. Indeed, with a combination of rain-fed rice fields, the retreating, flood water or *tanub* system, burning the forest to create rice land and the planting of the rapidly growing 'floating' rice, non-irrigated techniques could bring in four crops at different times of the year.

If the *barays* at Angkor were not used for irrigation, how was rice grown? Aerial photographs have revealed many temple sites associated with small rectangular reservoirs and square plots, all on the same axis. These square enclosures are, beyond reasonable doubt, Angkorian rice fields. No such site has yet been dated, but there are strong grounds for suggesting that agriculture incorporated bunded fields for which, in an average year, rainfall was sufficient to produce satisfactory returns. The number of references to water buffaloes and at least one possible reference to a plough suggest that all the ingredients of modern rain-fed agriculture were in place during the period of Angkor from AD 800. There is also, as Acker has pointed out, the possibility that the many small tanks could have been used as sources of water in the face of difficult dry spells. If they were dug down below the water table, they would have been constantly replenished as water was drawn off.

The balance of evidence argues strongly against a large, centrally controlled irrigation system based on the *barays*. This removes the control of irrigation facilities from any explanation for the rise of royal power, or for the collapse of the state. What, then, was the purpose of the *barays*? If the temples represented Mount Meru, the reservoirs would become the surrounding oceans. Their symbolic role is likewise seen at other major state temples, such as Preah Khan of Kompong Svai and Banteay Chmar. The scale of the Angkor *barays* increased from the Indratataka, which covers 240 hectares, to the Yashodharatataka (1260 hectares) and the huge Western Baray (1680 hectares). It would be hard to conceive of a better way of projecting power and majesty than to construct such monuments to create heaven on earth. Nor would this parallel be lost on the pilgrim crossing the water to the temples located in the centre of each *baray*, there to worship the royal ancestors and return freed from sins. Anyone who has sat in the shade next to a reservoir during April, when the sun burns from a leaden sky, and felt the breeze off the water, will likewise approve of the merit gained by its creator.

The reign of Jayavarman VII appears like a final burst of energy before the decline. Thereafter, there was a sharp reduction in building, and inscriptions became a rarity. Several factors have been advanced to account for the changed situation, even if Angkor remained an impressive and vibrant centre when Zhou Daguan visited it. Groslier and Dumarçay have maintained that the decline reflects the failure of the irrigation system due to siltation and difficulties of maintenance. This now seems highly unlikely. It was during this period that the vigorous Thai kingdoms of Sukhothai and Ayutthaya posed a serious military threat from the west, culminating in the lengthy siege and the sacking of Angkor in 1431. Others have pointed out that the adoption of Theravada Buddhism, in place of the traditional worship of Shiva linked with the ancestors, not only preached social equality, but removed the need for state temples, meritorious donations and inscriptions.

While the proximity of the kingdom of Ayutthaya, and its destruction of Angkor, may have led to the final abandonment, it is important to stress that this did not signal the end of the kingdom of Cambodia. A move to the Mekong Valley and back to the heartland of Jayavarman I ensured that the state and its traditions were maintained. It may well have been that further changes to international trade patterns encouraged such a move, which has seen Phnom Penh, commanding the junction of four rivers, established as the new capital centre. The traditions of Angkor survive both in the person of the King of Cambodia and, equally, in the court rituals of the Chakri dynasty of Thailand. The factional rivalries that attended the accession of King Norodom Sihanoukvarman in 1941 could have been taken directly from the events of 1002–6. As Haing Ngor said before the rise of the Khmer Rouge, the Cambodian peasants thought of their king as a god.

The civilization of Angkor in wider perspective

General reviews of archaic states tend to concentrate upon intensely studied areas, such as Egypt, Mesopotamia or Meso-America. Occasionally, South-East Asia reaches centre stage for comparative purpose. Does it show similarities with the regions under intensive study? One of several problems with this comparative approach is that there are few authoritative descriptions of the state of Angkor that begin with its deep roots in the prehistoric past and continue to the abandonment of its great city. Those that do have only paid lip service to prehistory at best, and often present an entirely inaccurate portrayal. Cœdès, after a lifetime of dedication to the inscriptions, described the indigenous inhabitants, who in effect generated the civilization of Angkor, as Stone Age savages.

Recent syntheses of the origins of states in other parts of the world have identified several significant variables. Robert Carneiro, for example, has advanced six conditions for the emergence of a state from preceding chiefdoms. They revolve round the power to defeat neighbours and to incorporate them into a larger polity; the power to enslave prisoners; the power to take tribute; the ability to provide a corps of fighting men; and the ability to place supporters in control over conquered territory. There is considerable support for these propositions in recent instances of state formation assembled by Kent Flannery. The ritual and physical control of trade is a further variable, which recurs in many cases, while Henry Wright has noted how early stages in state formation are characterized by 'chiefly cycling': the ebb and flow of social complexity before the transition to the state has occurred. Joyce Marcus has taken up this theme in her dynamic model, noting the widespread finding in Meso-America that archaic states underwent phases of regional dominance and contraction. The Maya, for example, began as a collection of competing chiefdoms with cyclic rises and falls in power as the centre of gravity switched. In Mesopotamia, the rulers of Susa controlled a state covering a wide area from 3700 to 3200 BC, but during the late Uruk phase, it split into two competing groups. Is there, underlying these similar patterns, a recurrent difficulty in maintaining inegalitarian social systems?

Although the Maya of Meso-America and the Khmer of Angkor have from time to time been linked as lowland forest civilizations, there are in fact several basic differences. The latter benefited from that most adaptive and productive of grains, rice. The people of Angkor also possessed powerful draught animals and iron technology. Yet it is still possible to identify a number of consistencies with other emerging states. Even in the late Iron Age, there is some evidence for the crowding of settlements in the favoured low-lying river valleys of the southern Khorat plateau, linked with a surge in population. The only extensive excavation of one of these sites has shown that there was an abundance of iron weapons. Steps were also taken to control the flow of water well before such techniques were allegedly introduced by Indian traders. With the first Chinese accounts of the Mekong Delta region, we are able to read of wars for territorial gains, the incorporation of other groups into a single polity and the placement of a king's relatives in authority over the conquered.

Nor should the massive investment in canals linking the delta settlements be overlooked. If modern practice is any guide, these were used for drainage and rapid transport across a marshy land-scape. A further widespread feature of early trends towards state formation is the existence of drainage and agricultural improve-ments to maintain the loyalty of followers. This too is suggested by an early and important inscription from Go Thap.

Funan, the delta state, probably lasted for two or three centuries before it suffered from a change in international trade routes and the rise of powerful inland chiefs. The 250 years from AD 550 onwards in the riverine flood plains of the interior saw two dia-metrically opposing forces at work. The first involved high chiefs, overlords or kings attempting to control land and labour through force and the projection of a sacred persona. This was offset by other local leaders pursuing independence and their own push for regional hegemony. In this context, the cyclic rising and falling of competing overlords echoes similar sequences noted in the Near East and the Americas. Within this period, one does not need to look far to find evidence for growing social inequality. The very names are sufficient evidence; on the one hand, the Sanskrit title of a king meaning protégé of the great Indra, and on the other hand, workers with Khmer names meaning dog, stinker, black monkey and arse.

Within this period of competition and endemic conflict, the inscriptions of Jayavarman I reflect a breakthrough in state forma-tion, with his appointment of state officials and the creation of at least three and probably four tiers of settlement hierarchy. Yet his successors are only recorded for one generation before the epigraphic record for this dynasty fell silent.

Arthur Demarest has recently suggested that Mayan kings were not greatly concerned with agriculture or its intensification, nor with trade other than that involving symbols of ritual potency, such as quetzal feathers and jade. This, he stressed, emphasizes the importance they attached to religion. The Maya regarded their rulers as the means of communicating with the divine world of the gods and ancestors, and as the symbolic axis of the universe. This helps us understand their investment in awe-inspiring temples, symbolically important façades, stelae commemorating accession to rule, genealogies and victories, and their concern to control access to symbols of office. On the reverse of the coin, the failure of a harvest or a military defeat would soon remove the aura of divinity.

This key issue, which Demarest has proposed for the Maya, finds parallels in Angkor. It has been argued that the kings of Angkor did not control a massive, centralized irrigation system based on their undoubted skill in hydraulic engineering. Angkor might have seemed an oriental Venice, but there is insufficient evidence to follow Groslier in advocating a kingdom based on irrigated rice. The weight of evidence is more in favour of a decentralized system, in which grandee families controlled labour for the production of rain-fed rice in small bunded fields, supplemented by floating or flood-retreat rice or rice grown in burnt over woodland where appropriate. This does not rule out some local and small-scale networks of channels to bring water to rice fields if the monsoon faltered, but this is not the royally inspired hydraulic civilization conceived by Groslier and Dumarçay and assumed by many others.

As with the Maya, we are left to ponder how kings maintained their grip on power. In his review of the South-East Asian 'galactic polity', Stanley Tambiah has reached the same conclusion as Demarest, but his argument is based in the main upon Siamese and Javan examples, with little consideration of Angkor. The epigraphic and architectural record for Cambodia, however, provides sufficient information to take his views seriously. He emphasized in particular the capital as the *axis mundi*, the symbolic centre of the universe. This is self-evident in the inscriptions and architectural remains of Angkor. He stressed the importance of royal sacred power and adherence to *dharma*, the sacred moral law. Here too, we find numerous allusions to the divine nature of the king, whose name was joined with that of Shiva in the golden *linga* in his temple. In terms of architecture, Angkor is, par excellence, the outstanding example of building in the name of majesty and sacred power. The role of the king in interceding with the deified ancestors, and ordering the construction of reservoirs containing temples that literally removed a person's sins and assured a better rebirth, again reflects the importance of ritual authority.

Yet there was a darker side. However many insignia of high status were handed down, however much land was donated, however many roads and bridges were constructed, there was still the problem of controlling distant provinces and court factions. So the civilization of Angkor joins its peers elsewhere in exhibiting chronic instability in times of central weakness, and a tendency to fragment and contract with outside pressure. Yet, despite its abandonment in 1431, the symbol of Angkor has survived and grown over the years. Through a century of colonial rule, and the agony of the Khmer Rouge, the civilization of Angkor continues to unify and inspire Khmer and foreigner alike.

GLOSSARY

acarya A spiritual guide or teacher, instructor of religious mysteries.

-aditya A name suffix meaning rising sun.

Angkor A name derived from the Sanskrit word *nagara*, meaning a holy city. It appears in Thai as *nakhon* and in Cham as *nagar*.

apsara A Sanskrit word for a celestial female dancer attentive to kings, gods and heroes.

ashrama A retreat for ascetics or hermits who devote themselves to preparing for the next life.

avatar A word derived from the Sanskrit term for the incarnation of a deity in a different form.

Banteay A Khmer name for a fortress or citadel. It has been applied to temples because of their encircling walls.

baray A Sanskrit word for a reservoir.

bodhisattva Meaning enlightened in Sanskrit, this describes one who, on the brink of full enlightenment, forgoes this stage to help others.

Brahma A god forming part of a trinity (with Shiva and Vishnu) who was the creator of the world and universe.

Buddha Gautama Siddhartha was the first Buddha, meaning one who has attained spiritual enlightenment. He lived in the sixth century BC.

chakravartin A title for the supreme king or universal overlord, derived from the Sankrit term for one who turns the wheel of the law.

Champa/the Chams A people speaking an Austronesian language who occupied southern coastal Vietnam and were often enganged in war with the Khmer.

167

Chenla A Chinese name given to the states that occupied Cambodia from about AD 550 to 800.

churning of the ocean milk In this Hindu myth, gods and demons pull on Vasuki, a snake coiled round Mount Mahendra, to churn the ocean of milk and produce the elixir of immortality.

-deva Masculine, heavenly or divine.

-devi Female, heavenly or divine.

devaraja A controversial term meaning literally the god who is king. The cult was described as originating in the reign of Jayavarman II in a much later inscription, and its importance has probably been exaggerated.

Dhuli jen vrah kamraten an The highest title a king could bestow. *Dhuli jen*: literally, dust of the feet.

fan A title for overlords or kings of Funan recorded in Chinese histories. It is probably the same word as *pon* in Khmer.

Funan The name originating in Chinese reports for a state that developed in the Mekong Delta during the first few centuries AD.

Garuda The mythical creature, half bird, half man, who carried Vishnu on his back.

gopura A Sanskrit word for an entrance pavilion and gateway to a temple.

guru A spiritual guide.

Harihara A god with the combined image of Shiva and Vishnu.

hotar A priest.

Indra The Hindu god of war and tempests, with special reference to the east.

-isvara A name suffix, meaning incorporating qualities of Shiva.

jaya A name prefix, from the Sanskrit word for victory.

jyan A measure by weight.

kamratan A high religious title, more exalted than a *kamsten*.

kamsten A religious title.

khleang A monument whose name means 'emporium' but whose purpose is still unclear.

khlon glan The title given to the chief of the warehouse.

khlon karya The chief of corvée labour.

khlon visaya An official in charge of land ownership.

knum A junior kinsman, also a slave.

kpon Ancestral or local deities, often female.

Krishna An incarnation of the god Vishnu.

Lakshmi The consort of Shiva and a goddess of beauty, originating in the churning of the ocean of milk.

Lokesvara A *bodhisattva*, compassionately concerned with mankind.

mantrin A king's counsellor or minister.

mebon An island temple.

Mount Meru The home of the gods, a mountain at the centre of the universe.

mratan An official appointed by the king in central and regional administration.

mratan klon The official appointed to govern a place or region.

mratan kurun An official appointed to rule a region, higher in status than a *mratan klon*.

naga A multi-headed cobra, seen mythically as the origin and protector of the Angkorian state.

Nandi A bull, the mount for Shiva.

pala A measure by weight.

phnom The Khmer word for a hill or mountain.

pon A hereditary title for a highly ranked member of society, usually a local leader who had authority to endow land and livestock. The title *pon* passed from a man to his sister's son. It was used until the early eighth century AD.

preah The Khmer word for sacred or holy. *Preah khan* means sacred sword.

praman An administrative unit or territory under the king's jurisdiction.

raja King.

rajakulamahamantri A title meaning great adviser.

Rama An incarnation of Vishnu and a folk hero who plays the leading role in the Indian epic story that describes his adventures, the *Ramayana*.

Shiva A major Hindu god of creation and destruction.

sresthin A middle grade official.

sruk A small territorial division, possibly the size of a village.

Surya- A name prefix meaning the sun.

tamrvac Centrally appointed agents for the government in the provinces.

tanub A dyke.

vap An honorific title meaning father.

-varman A name suffix meaning shield or protector.

vavihamika The owner of a reservoir in Sri Lanka.

visaya A territorial area.

Vishnu The Hindu god of compassion and preservation.

vrah guru Senior minister with particular responsibility for religious foundations.

vrah kamraten an A divine title given to royal leaders.

vyapara An official appointed by the king to establish and fix boundaries.

yoni The female genitals, represented at the base of the *linga*.

References for Further Reading

Abbreviations used

AP   Asian Perspectives
BEFEO *Bulletin de l'École Française d'Extrême-Orient*
EFEO   École Française d'Extrême-Orient
PEFEO *Publications de l'École Française d'Extrême-Orient*
SOAS   School of Oriental and African Studies

General

Cœdès, G. 1968. *The Indianized States of Southeast Asia*, University of Hawaii, Honolulu.
Giteau, M. 1965. *Khmer Sculpture and the Angkor Civilisation*, Thames and Hudson, London.
Jacques, C. 1997. *Angkor, Cities and Temples*, River Books, Bangkok.
Le Bonheur, A. 1995. *Of Gods, Kings and Men*, Serindia, London.
Mazzeo, D. and Antonini, C.S. 1978. *Monuments of Civilization: Ancient Cambodia*, Grosset and Dunlap, New York.

Chapter 1: Introduction: 'One of the Marvels of the World', pp. 1–12

Alpers, E.A. 1969. 'Trade, state and society among the Yao in the nineteenth century', *Journal of African History*, X (3): 405–20.
Flannery, K.V. 1998. 'The ground plans of archaic states' in Feinman, G.M. and Marcus, J. (eds), *Archaic States*, pp. 15–57, School of American Research Press, Santa Fe.
Flannery, K. 1999. 'Process and agency in early state formation', *Cambridge Archaeological Journal*, 9: 3–21.

Flood, G. 1996. *An Introduction to Hinduism*, Cambridge University Press, Cambridge.

Groslier, B.-P. 1958. 'Angkor et le Cambodge au XVIᵉ Siècle d'après les Sources Portugaises et Espagnoles', *Annales du Musée Guimet*, 63, Paris.

Groslier, B.-P. 1979. 'La Cité Hydraulique Angkorienne: exploitation ou surexploitation du sol?' *BEFEO*, LVI: 161–202.

Ribadeneyra, F.M. de. 1601. *Historia de Las Islas del Archipelago y Reynos de la Gran China*. G. Graells, Barcelona.

Tambiah, S.J. 1977. 'The galactic polity: the structure of traditional kingdoms in Southeast Asia', *Annals of the New York Academy of Sciences*, 293: 69–97.

Chapter 2: The Prehistoric Period in South-East Asia, pp. 13–22

Boulbet, J. 1979. *Le Phnom Kulen et sa Région*, EFEO, Paris.

Cœdès, G. 1931. 'Études Cambodgiennes', *BEFEO*, XXXI: 2–23.

Cœdès, G. 1937. 'A new inscription from Fu-Nan', *Journal of the Greater India Society*, 4: 117–21.

Delvert, J. 1994. *Le Paysan Cambodgien*, L'Harmattan, Paris.

Glover, I.C. 1989. *Early Trade Between India and Southeast Asia: a Link in the Development of a World Trading System*, University of Hull Centre for Southeast Asian Studies, Occasional Paper no. 16, Hull.

Higham, C.F.W. and Lu, T.L.-D. 1998. 'The origins and dispersal of rice cultivation', *Antiquity*, 72: 867–77.

Higham, C.F.W. and Thosarat, R. 1994. *Prehistoric Thailand: from First Settlement to Sukhothai*, River Books, Bangkok.

Higham, C.F.W. and Kijngam, A. (eds). 1984. *Prehistoric Excavations in Northeast Thailand: Excavations at Ban Na Di, Ban Chiang Hian, Ban Muang Phruk, Ban Sangui, Non Noi and Ban Kho Noi*, British Archaeological Reports, International Series 231 (i–iii), Oxford.

Higham, C.F.W. and Thosarat, R. (eds). 1988. *The Excavation of Nong Nor, a Prehistoric Site in Central Thailand*, Oxbow Books, Oxford and University of Otago Studies in Prehistoric Anthropology, no. 18, Dunedin.

Moore, E. and Freeman, A. 1998. 'Circular sites at Angkor: a radar scattering model', *Journal of the Siam Society*, 85: 107–19.

Nitta, E. 1991. 'Archaeological study on the ancient iron-smelting and salt-making industries in the northeast of Thailand: preliminary report on the excavations of Non Yang and Ban Don Phlong', *Journal of Southeast Asian Archaeology*, 11: 1–46.

Pigott, V.C., Weiss, A.D. and Natapintu, S. 1997. 'The archaeology of copper production: excavations in the Khao Wong Prachan Valley, Central Thailand' in Ciarla, R. and Rispoli, F. (eds), *South-East Asian Archaeology 1992*, Istituto Italiano per l'Africa e l'Oriente, Rome.

Sedov, L.A. 1978. 'Angkor: society and state' in Claessen, H.J.M. and Skalník, P. (eds), *The Early State*, pp. 111–30, Mouton, The Hague.

Sørensen, P. 1988. 'The kettledrums from Ongbah Cave, Kanchanaburi Province' in Sørensen, P. (ed.), *Archaeological Excavations in Thailand: Surface Finds and Minor Excavations*, pp. 95–116, Scandinavian Institute of Asian Studies, Occasional Paper no. 1, Copenhagen.

Chapter 3: The Earliest Civilization in South-East Asia, pp. 23–35

Dao Linh Con, 1997. 'The Oc Eo burial group recently excavated at Go Thap (Dong Thap Province, Viet Nam)', P.-Y. in Manguin (ed), *Southeast Asian Archaeology 1994*, pp. 111–16, Centre for Southeast Asian Studies, University of Hull, Hull.

Garnier, F. 1871. 'Voyage des Hollandais en Cambodge et Laos en 1644', *Bulletin de la Société de Géographie*, II–19: 251–89.

Hall, K. 1985. *Maritime Trade and State Development in Early Southeast Asia*, University of Hawaii Press, Honolulu.

Jacques, C. [n.d.] *Corpus des Inscriptions du Pays Khmer 1: Inscriptions Préangkoriennes Nommant un Roi*, International Academy of Indian Culture, New Delhi.

Jacques, C. 1978. '"Funan", "Zhenla": the reality concealed by these Chinese views of Indochina' in Smith, R.B. and Watson, W. (eds), *Early South East Asia*, pp. 443–56, Oxford University Press, Kuala Lumpur.

Le Xuan Diem, Dao Linh Con and Vo Si Khai, 1995. *Van Hoa Oc Eo Nhung Kham Pha Moi*, Nha Xuat Ban Khoa Hoc Xa Hoi, Hanoi.

Malleret, L. 1959–63. *L'Archéologie du Delta du Mékong*, EFEO, Paris.

Manguin, P.-Y. 1996. 'Southeast Asian shipping in the Indian Ocean during the first millennium A.D.' in Ray, H.P. and Salles, J.-F. (eds), *Tradition and Archaeology: Early Maritime Contacts in the Indian Ocean*, pp. 181–98, Manohar, New Delhi.

Stark, M.T., Griffin, P.B., Chuch Phoeurn, Ledgerwood, J., Dega, M., Mortland, C., Dowling, N., Bayman, J.M., Bong Sovath, Tea Van, Chhan Chamroven and Latinis, K. 1999. 'Results of the 1995–6 archaeological field investigations at Angkor Borei, Cambodia', *AP*, 38 (1): 7–36.

Wheatley, P. 1983. *Nagara and Commandery: Origins of the Southeast Asian Urban Traditions*, University of Chicago, Department of Geography, Research Paper 207–8, Chicago.

Chapter 4: The Early Kingdoms of Chenla, pp. 36–52

Bénisti, M. 1970. *Rapports entre le Premier Art Khmer et l'Art Indien*, *PEFEO*, Mémoires Archéologiques V, Paris.

Boisselier, J. 1955. 'La Statuaire Khmère et son Evolution', *PEFEO* 37.

Boulbet, J. and Dagens, B. 1973. 'Les sites archéologiques de la region du Bhnam Gulen (Phnom Kulen)', *Arts Asiatiques*, 27: 68 pp.

Jacob, J.M. 1979. 'Pre-Angkor Cambodia: evidence from the inscriptions in Khmer concerning the common people and their environment' in Smith, R.B. and Watson, W. (eds), *Early South East Asia*, pp. 406–26, Oxford University Press, Kuala Lumpur.

Jacques, C. 1986a. 'Le pays Khmer avant Angkor', *Journal des Savants*, 1986: 59–95.

Jacques, C. 1986b. 'New data on the VII–VIIIth centuries in the Khmer lands' in Glover, I.C. and Glover, E. (eds), *Southeast Asian Archaeology 1986*, BAR International Series 561, Oxford.

Kulke, H. 1986. 'The early and the imperial kingdoms in Southeast Asian history' in Marr, D.G. and Milner, A.C. (eds), *Southeast Asia in the 9th to 14th Centuries*, pp. 1–22, Institute of Southeast Asian Studies, Singapore, and Research School of Pacific Studies, ANU Canberra.

Parmentier, H. 1927. *L'Art Khmer Primitif*, EFEO, Paris.

Renfrew, A.C. 1979. 'Systems collapse as social transformations: catastrophe and anastrophe in early state societies' in Renfrew, A.C. and Cooke, K.L. (eds), *Transformations: Mathematical Approaches to Culture Change*, pp. 481–506, Academic Press, London.

Vickery, M. 1986. 'Some remarks on early state formation in Cambodia' in Marr, D.G. and Milner, A.C. (eds), *Southeast Asia in the 9th to 14th Centuries*, pp. 95–115, Institute of Southeast Asian Studies, Singapore, and Research School of Pacific Studies, ANU Canberra.

Vickery, M. 1994. 'What and where was Chenla?' in Bizot, F. (ed.), *Recherchés Nouvelles sur le Cambodge*, pp. 197–212, EFEO, Paris.

Vickery, M. 1998. *Society, Economics and Politics in Pre-Angkor Cambodia*, The Centre for East Asian Cultural Studies for Unesco, Tokyo.

Chapter 5: The Dynasty of Jayavarman II, pp. 53–90

Aymonier, E. 1900. *Le Cambodge*, E. Leroux, Paris.

Bizoy, F. 1994. (ed.) *Nouvelles Recherchés sur le Cambodge*, pp. 197–212, EFEO, Paris.

Briggs, L.P. 1951. 'The Ancient Khmer Empire', *Transactions of the American Philosophical Society*, n.s. 41, Philadelphia.

Bruguier, B. 1994. 'Le Prasat Ak Yum, état des connaissances' in Bizoy, F. (ed.), *Nouvelles Recherchés sur le Cambodge*, pp. 273–96, EFEO, Paris.

Cœdès, G. 1936–66. *Inscriptions de Cambodge* (8 vols), EFEO, Collections de textes et documents sur l'Indochine III, Paris.

Cœdès, G. and Dupont, P. 1943–6. 'Les Stèles de Sdok Kak Thom, Phnom Sandak et Prah Vihear', *BEFEO*, XLIII: 56–154.

Goloubew, V. 1933. 'Le Phnom Bakhen, la ville de Yasovarman', *BEFEO*, XXXIII: 319–44.

Goloubew, V. 1936. 'Reconnaissances aériennes au Cambodge', *BEFEO*, XXXVI: 465–77.

Jacques, C. 1972. 'La carrière de Jayavarman II', *BEFEO*, LIX: 205–20.

Jacques, C. 1997. *Angkor, Cities and Temples*, River Books, Bangkok.

Kulke, H. 1978. *The Devaraja Cult*, Data Paper no. 108, Southeast Asia Program, Dept. of Asian Studies, Cornell University.

Marchal, H. 1937. 'Notes sur le dégagement de Prasat Kok Po', *BEFEO*, XXXVII: 361–78.

Ricklefs, M.C. 1967. 'Land and the law in the epigraphy of tenth-century Cambodia', *Journal of the Royal Asiatic Society*, XXVI: 411–20.

Roveda, V. 1997. *Khmer Mythology*, River Books, Bangkok.

Sahai, S. 1970. *Les Institutions Politiques et L'Organisation Administrative du Cambodge Ancien (VI–XIIIth Siècles)*, PEFEO, LXXV.

Stern, P. 1936. 'Le Style de Kulen', *BEFEO*, XXXVI: 111–49.

Vickery, M. 1997. [review article] 'What to do about the Khmers', *Journal of Southeast Asian Studies*, 27 (2): 389–404.

Chapter 6: The Dynasty of the Sun Kings, pp. 91–106

Cœdès, G. 1913a. 'La stèle de Palhal', *BEFEO*, XIII (6): 27–36.

Cœdès, G. 1913b. 'Le serment des fonctionnaires de Suryavarman I', *BEFEO*, XIII (6): 11–17.

Corbin, P. 1988. *La Fouille du Sras-Srang à Angkor*, EFEO, Collections de Textes et Documents sur l'Indochine, Mémoires Archéologiques XVII.

De Mestier du Bourg, H. 1970. 'La première moitié du XI° siècle au Cambodge: Suryavarman 1ᵉʳ, sa vie et quelques aspects des institutions à son époque', *Journal Asiatique*, 258 (3–4): 281–314.

Delaporte, L. 1880. *Voyage au Cambodge. L'Architecture Khmère*, Paris.

Engelhardt, R.A. 1996. 'New directions for archaeological research on the Angkor Plain: the use of remote sensing technology for research into ancient Khmer environmental engineering', *Bulletin of the Indo-Pacific Prehistory Association*, 14: 151–60.

Hall, K. 1975. 'Khmer commercial developments and foreign contacts under Suryavarman I', *Journal of Economic and Social History of the Orient*, 18: 318–36.

Mauger, H. 1940. 'Prah Khan de Kompon Svay', *BEFEO*, XXXIX: 197–220.

Moore, E. and Siribhadra, S. 1992. *Palaces of the Gods: Khmer Art and Architecture in Thailand*, River Books, Bangkok.

Vickery, M. 1985. 'The reign of Suryavarman I and royal factionalism at Angkor', *Journal of Southeast Asian Studies* 16 (2): 226–44.

Chapter 7: The Dynasty of Mahidharapura, pp. 107–142

Aoyagi, Y. 1999. *Excavation of Tani pottery kiln site in Angkor area*, Report on the 4th excavation of pottery kiln sites, Report to the Unesco Cultural Commission, Phnom Penh.

Argensola, B.L. de, 1609. *Conquista de las Islas Malucas*. A. Martin, Madrid.

Aymonier, E. 1900–1903. *La Cambodge*. Ernest Léroux, Paris.

Cœdès, G. 1906. 'La stèle de Ta-Prohm', *BEFEO*, VI (1906): 44–81.

Cœdès, G. 1913. 'Note sur l'Iconographie de Ben Mala', *BEFEO*, XII (2): 23–8.

Cœdès, G. 1929. 'Nouvelles données chronologiques et généalogiques sur la dynastie de Mahidharapura', *BEFEO*, XXIX: 297–330.

Cœdès, G. 1941. 'La stèle du Prah Khan d'Angkor', *BEFEO*, XLI: 255–301.

Cœdès, G. 1947–50. 'L'Épigraphie de monuments de Jayavarman VII', *BEFEO*, XLIV: 97–119.

Cœdès, G. 1966. *Angkor: an Introduction*, Oxford University Press, Hong Kong.

Dagens, B. 1998. [review of Mannika, E., 1996, *Angkor Wat: Time, Space and Kingship*], *BEFEO*, LXXXV: 500.

De Mecquenem, J. 1913. 'Les bâtiments annexés de Ben Mala', *BEFEO*, XII (2): 1–22.

Dufour, M.H. 1901. 'Documents photographique sur les fêtes ayant accompagné la coupe solonnelle des cheveux du Prince Chandalekha fils de Noroudam, en Mai 1901, à Phnom Penh, recueillis et annotés', *BEFEO*, I: 231–4.

Finot, L. 1925. 'Inscriptions d'Ankor', *BEFEO*, XXV: 289–407.

Groslier, B.-P. 1981. *Introduction to the ceramic wares of Angkor. Khmer Ceramics: 9th–14th Century*, Southeast Asian Ceramic Society, Singapore.

Jacques, C. 1999. *Angkor*. Könemann, Cologne.

Mannika, E. 1996. *Angkor Wat: Time, Space and Kingship*, Allen and Unwin, St Leonards.

Parmentier, H. 1910. 'Les bas-reliefs de Banteai-Chmar', *BEFEO*, X: 205–22.

Trouvé, G. 1933. 'Chronique', *BEFEO*, XXXIII: 1120–7.

Trouvé, G. 1935. 'Chronique', *BEFEO*, XXXV: 483–6.

Zhou Daguan. 1993. *The Customs of Cambodia*, The Siam Society, Bangkok.

Chapter 8: The Civilization of Angkor, pp. 143–166

Acker, R.L. 1997. *New Geographic Tests of the Hydraulic Thesis at Angkor*, M.A. Dissertation, School of Oriental and African Studies, London.

Briggs, L.P. 1951. 'The Ancient Khmer Empire', *Transactions of the American Philosophical Society*, 4 (i): 1–295.

Carneiro, R.L. 1992. 'Point counterpoint: Ecology and ideology in the development of New World civilizations' in Dermarest, A.A. and Conrad, G.W. (eds), *Ideology and Pre-Columbian Civilizations*, pp. 175–204. School of American Research Press, Santa Fe.

Claessen, H.J.M. and Skalník, P. (eds). 1978. *The Early State*, Mouton, The Hague.

Claessen, H.J.M. and Van der Velde, P. (eds). 1987a. *Early State Dynamics*, Brill, Leiden.

Claessen, H.J.M. and Van der Velde, P. (eds). 1987b. *Early State Economics*, Transaction Publishers, New Jersey.

Delvert, J. 1961. Le Paysan Cambodgien. *Le Monde d'Outre Mer Passé et Present*. Première Série No. 10, École Practique des Hautes Études, Sorbonne, Paris.

Demarest, A.A. 1992. 'Ideology in ancient Maya cultural evolution: the dynamics of galactic polities' in Demarest, A.A. and Conrad, G.W. (eds), *Ideology and Pre-Columbian Civilizations*, pp. 135–57, School of American Research Press, Santa Fe.

Demarest, A.A. and Wright, H.T. 1993. 'The culture history of Madagascar', *Journal of World Prehistory*, 7: 417–66.

Dumarçay, J. 1998. *The Site of Angkor*, Oxford University Press, Oxford.

Feinman, G.M. 1998. 'Scale and social organization: perspectives on the archaic state' in Feinman, G.M. and Marcus, J. (eds), *Archaic States*, pp. 95–133, School of American Research Press, Santa Fe.

Feinman, G.M. and Marcus, J. (eds), 1998. *Archaic States*, School of American Research Press, Santa Fe.

Flannery, K. 1999. 'Process and agency in early state formation', *Cambridge Archaeological Journal*, 9: 3–21.

Gesick, L. 1983. 'Centers, symbols, and hierarchies: essays on the classical states of southeast Asia', *Southeast Asia Studies Monograph Series*, no. 26, Yale University Press, New Haven.

Gunawardana, R.A.L.H. 1981. 'Social function and political power: a case study of state formation in irrigation society' in Claessen, H.J.M. and Skalník, P. (eds), *The Study of the State*, pp. 133–54, Mouton, The Hague.

Hagesteijn, R. 1987. 'The Angkor state: rise, fall and in between' in Claessen, H.J.M. and Van der Velde, P. (eds), pp. 154–69, *Early State Dynamics*, Brill, Leiden.

Marcus, H. 1998. 'The peaks and valleys of ancient states' in Feinman, G.M. and Marcus, J. (eds), *Archaic States*, pp. 59–94, School of American Research Press, Santa Fe.

Ngor Haing, S. 1988. *Surviving the Killing Fields*, Chatto and Windus, London.

Osborne, M. 1994. *Sihanouk: Prince of Light, Prince of Darkness*, University of Hawaii Press, Honolulu.

Pelliot, P. 1902. 'Mémoires sur les coutumes du Cambodge', *BEFEO*, II: 123–77.

Stott, P. 1992. 'Angkor: shifting the hydraulic paradigm' in Rigg, J. (ed.), *The Gift of Water*, pp. 47–57, SOAS, London.

Tambiah, S.J. 1977. 'The galactic polity: the structure of traditional kingdoms in Southeast Asia', *Annals of the New York Academy of Sciences*, 293: 69–97.

Van Liere, W.J. 1980. 'Traditional water management in the lower Mekong Basin', *World Archaeology*, 11 (3): 265–80.

Winzeler, R. 1976. 'Ecology, culture, social organization and state formation in Southeast Asia', *Current Anthropology*, 17: 623–40.

Wright, H.T. 1984. 'Prestate political formations' in Earle, T.K. (ed.), *On the Evolution of Complex Societies*, pp. 43–77, Undena, Malibu.

Wright, H.T. 1998. 'Uruk states in southwestern Iran' in Feinman, G.M. and Marcus, J. (eds), *Archaic States*, pp. 173–97, School of American Research Press, Santa Fe.

Wright, H.T. and Johnson, G.A. 1975. 'Population, exchange, and early state formation in southwestern Iran', *American Anthropologist*, 77: 267–89.

INDEX